# Chaucer

# THE
# *Wife of Bath's*
# PROLOGUE AND TALE

Edited by Valerie Allen and David Kirkham

CAMBRIDGE
UNIVERSITY PRESS

The publishers would like to thank Helen Cooper and Alexander Murray for their help in the preparation of this edition.

CAMBRIDGE UNIVERSITY PRESS
Cambridge, New York, Melbourne, Madrid, Cape Town,
Singapore, São Paulo, Delhi, Tokyo, Mexico City

Cambridge University Press
The Edinburgh Building, Cambridge CB2 8RU, UK

www.cambridge.org
Information on this title: www.cambridge.org/9780521595070

First published 1998
14th printing 2012

Printed in the United Kingdom at the University Press, Cambridge

*A catalogue record for this publication is available from the British Library*

ISBN 978-0-521-59507-0 Paperback

Prepared for publication by Paren & Stacey Editorial Consultants
Designed and formatted by Geoffrey Wadsley
Illustrated by Adam Stower
Picture research by Jane Taylor

*Thanks are due to the following for permission to reproduce photographs:*
Ancient Art and Architecture Collection, page 32; The Bodleian Library, University of Oxford, MS Douce 195, folio 116V, page 36; Bridgeman Art Library, London, pages 20, *The Wilton Diptych*, National Gallery and 102, *Portrait of Geoffrey Chaucer*, British Library; British Library, pages 107*t*, MS Royal, 16 G V, folio 54V and 109, MS Sloane 2435, folio 44V; Dover Publications/Pat Hodgson Library, page 42; Getty Images, page 7; Magnum Photos, page 100; Mary Evans Picture Library, pages 12, 43, 54 and 99; JCD Smith, pages 107*b* and 110

For cover photograph: Canterbury Tales: Wife of Bath *Ellesmere Manuscript, (Facsimile Edition 1911),* Private Collection/Bridgeman Art Library, London

# Contents

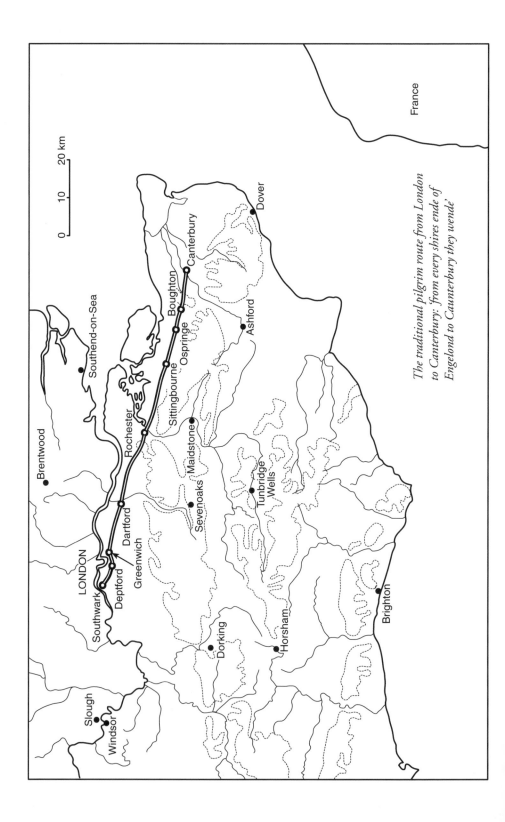

The traditional pilgrim route from London to Canterbury: 'from every shires ende of Engelond to Caunterbury they wende'

0   10   20 km

France

Dover

Canterbury

Boughton

Ospringe

Ashford

Sittingbourne

Southend-on-Sea

Rochester

Maidstone

Brentwood

Sevenoaks

Tunbridge Wells

Dartford

Greenwich

Deptford

LONDON

Southwark

Horsham

Dorking

Brighton

Slough

Windsor

# Introduction

The first encounter with a page of Chaucer in its original form can be a disconcerting experience. Initially, few words look familiar. Even when the meaning has been puzzled out, the reader is faced with an account of people who lived and died in a world very different from our own. The fourteenth century seems very far away, and you might be forgiven for thinking that *The Canterbury Tales* are 'too difficult'.

The aim of this series is, therefore, to introduce you to the world of Chaucer in a way that will make medieval language and life as accessible as possible. With this in mind, we have adopted a layout in which each right-hand page of text is headed by a brief summary of content, and faced by a left-hand page offering a glossary of more difficult words and phrases as well as commentary notes dealing with style, characterisation and other relevant information. There are illustrations, and suggestions for ways in which you might become involved in the text to help make it come alive.

If initial hurdles are lowered in this way, Chaucer's wit and irony, his ability to suggest character and caricature, and his delight in raising provocative and challenging issues from various standpoints, can more readily be appreciated and enjoyed. There is something peculiarly delightful in discovering that someone who lived six hundred years ago had a sense of humour and a grasp of personalities and relationships as fresh and relevant today as it was then.

Each tale provides material for fruitful discussion of fourteenth century attitudes and contemporary parallels. It is important to realise that the views expressed by the teller of any one tale are not necessarily Chaucer's own. Many of the activities suggested are intended to make you aware of the multiplicity of voices and attitudes in *The Canterbury Tales*. A considerable part of the enjoyment of the tales comes from awareness of the tongue-in-cheek presence of the author, who allows his characters to speak for themselves, thereby revealing their weaknesses and obsessions.

Essential information contained in each book includes a brief explanation of what *The Canterbury Tales* are, followed by some hints on handling the language. There is then a brief introduction to the teller of the relevant story, his or her portrait from the General Prologue, and an initial investigation into the techniques Chaucer uses to presents characters.

The left-hand page commentaries give information applicable to the text. Finally, each book offers a full list of pilgrims, further information on Chaucer's own life and works, some background history, and greater discussion of specific medieval issues. Suggestions for essays and themes to be explored are also included. On page 112 there is a relatively short glossary of the words most frequently encountered in the text, to supplement the more detailed glossary on each page.

Chaucer's tales are witty, clever and approachable, and raise interesting parallels with life today. His manipulation of the short story form is masterly. We hope this edition brings *The Canterbury Tales* alive and allows you to appreciate Chaucer's art with ease and enjoyment.

# What are The Canterbury Tales?

They are a collection of stories, loosely linked together, apparently told by a variety of storytellers with very different characters and from different social classes. In fact, both the storytellers and the tales are the creation of one man, Geoffrey Chaucer. Chaucer imagines a group of pilgrims, setting off from the Tabard Inn one spring day on the long journey from London to the shrine of St Thomas à Becket in Canterbury – a journey that on horseback would take about four days.

To make time pass more pleasantly the pilgrims agree to tell stories to one another. Chaucer begins by introducing his pilgrims to the reader, in descriptions which do much to reveal the characters, vices and virtues of each individual. We learn more from the way each person introduces his or her tale, still more from the tales themselves and the way in which each one is told, and even further information is offered by the manner in which some pilgrims react to what others have to say. By this means Chaucer provides a witty, penetrating insight into the attitudes, weaknesses, virtues and preoccupations of English men and women of the fourteenth century. Some of their behaviour and interests may seem very strange to modern readers; at other times they seem just like us.

## THE TALES

Although the complete text of *The Canterbury Tales* no longer exists, enough remains for us to appreciate the richness of texture and ironical comment Chaucer wove into his tapestry of fourteenth century life. The Tales themselves are quite simple – medieval audiences did not expect original plots, but rather clever or unexpected ways of telling stories that might already be known in another form. Chaucer's audiences of educated friends, witty and urbane courtiers, perhaps the highest aristocracy, and even the king and queen, were clearly able to appreciate his skills to the full. Story-telling was a leisurely process, since reading was a social rather than a private activity, and, since many people could not read, Chaucer would expect the Tales to be read aloud. You could try to read them like this – you will find advice on pronunciation on page 9 – and you will discover they become still more lively and dramatic when spoken rather than just read on the page.

Most of the Tales include aspects of at least one of the following categories of tales familiar to Chaucer's audience.

**Courtly romances**  These courtly love affairs were for the upper classes. They often told of unrequited love from a distance, the male lover suffering sleepless nights of anguish, pining away, writing poetry, serenading his beloved with love songs and performing brave feats of noble daring. Meanwhile the beloved (but untouchable) lady would sit in her bower and sew, walk in her castle gardens, set her lover impossible tasks to accomplish, and give him a scarf or handkerchief as a keepsake. Chaucer enjoys poking gentle fun at the rarefied atmosphere of such stories.

**Fabliaux**  Extended jokes or tricks, these are often bawdy, and usually full of sexual innuendo.

*The destination of the pilgrims – Canterbury Cathedral today*

**Fables** These are tales that make a moral point, often using animals as characters.

**Sermons** Sermons were stories with a moral message. Since 95 per cent of society could not read, sermons had to be good, interesting and full of dramatic story-telling. The line between a good story and a good sermon was very thin indeed. Usually there was an abstract theme (gluttony, avarice, pride) and much use was made of biblical and classical parallels or *exempla* to underline the preacher's point.

**Confessions** The story-tellers often look back over their own lives, revealing faults and unhappinesses to the audience. This aspect is usually introduced in the teller's prologue to the actual story.

The Tales vary widely in content and tone, since medieval stories, Chaucer's included, were supposed both to instruct and to entertain. Many, like the Nun's Priest's Tale, have an underlying moral; some, such as the Pardoner's Tale, are highly dramatic; and others, like those told by the Knight and the Squire, have their origins firmly in the courtly love tradition. But many are more complex than this suggests: Chaucer includes stories as sentimental as that of the Prioress, and as crude and bawdy as those of the Miller and the Reeve.

The device of using different characters to tell different tales allows Chaucer to distance himself from what is being said, and to disguise the fact that he controls the varied and opinionated voices of his creations. He can pretend, for instance, to have no way of preventing the drunken Miller from telling his vulgar story about the carpenter's wife, and he can absolve himself from blame when the tellers become sexually explicit. A modern audience may find his frankness and openness about sex surprising, but it was understandable, for there was little privacy, even for the well-to-do, and sexual matters were no secret. The coarse satire of the fabliaux was as much enjoyed by Chaucer's 'gentil' audience as the more restrained romances.

7

# Chaucer's language

The unfamiliar appearance of a page of Chaucerian English often prevents students from pursuing their investigations any further. It does no good telling them that this man used language with a complexity and subtlety not found in any writer of English anywhere before him. They remain unimpressed. He looks incomprehensible.

In fact, with a little help, it does not take very long to master Chaucer's language. Much of the vocabulary is the same as, or at least very similar to, words we use today. On page 112 there is a glossary of the unfamiliar words most frequently used in this text, and these will quickly become familiar. Other words and phrases that could cause difficulties are explained on the pages facing the actual text.

The language of Chaucer is known as Middle English – a term covering English as it was written and spoken in the period roughly between 1150 and 1500. It is difficult to be more precise than this, for Middle English itself was changing and developing throughout that period towards 'modern' English.

Old English (Anglo-Saxon) was spoken and written until around 1066, the time of the Norman Conquest. This event put power in England into the hands of the Norman lords, who spoke their own brand of Norman French. Inevitably this became the language of the upper classes. The effect was felt in the church, for speedily the control of the monasteries and nunneries was given to members of the new French-speaking aristocracy. Since these religious houses were the seats of learning and centres of literacy, the effect on language was considerable. If you were a wealthy Anglo-Saxon, eager to get on in the world of your new over-lords, you learnt French. Many people were bi- or even trilingual: French was the language of the law courts and much international commerce; Latin was the language of learning (from elementary school to the highest levels of scholarship) and the church (from parish church services to the great international institution of the papacy).

Gradually, as inter-marriage between Norman French and English families became more common, the distinction between the two groups and the two languages became blurred. Many French words became absorbed into Old English, making it more like the language we speak today. In the thirteenth century King John lost control of his Norman lands, and, as hostility between England and France grew, a sense of English nationalism strengthened. In 1362 the English language was used for the first time in an English parliament. At the same time, Geoffrey Chaucer, a young ex-prisoner of war, was sharpening his pens and his wit, testing the potential for amusement, satire and beauty in this rich, infinitely variable, complex literary tool.

Although some Tales are partly, or entirely, in prose, *The Canterbury Tales* are written largely in rhyming iambic couplets. This form of regular metre and rhyme is flexible enough to allow Chaucer to write in a range of styles. He uses the couplet form to imitate colloquial speech as easily as philosophical debate. Most importantly, Chaucer wrote poetry 'for the ear': it is written for the listener, as much as for the reader. Rhyme and alliteration add emphasis and link ideas and objects together in a way that is satisfying for the audience. The words jog along as easily and comfortably as the imaginary pilgrims and their horses jogged to Canterbury.

# PRONUNCIATION

Chaucer spoke the language of London, of the king's court, but he was well aware of differences in dialect and vocabulary in other parts of the country. In the Reeve's Tale, for instance, he mocks the north country accents of two students. It is clear, therefore, that there were differences in pronunciation in the fourteenth century, just as there are today.

Having said that Chaucer wrote verse to be read aloud, students may be dismayed to find that they do not know how it should sound. There are two encouraging things to bear in mind. The first is that although scholars feel fairly sure they know something about how Middle English sounded, they cannot be certain, and a number of different readings can be heard. The second concerns the strong metrical and rhyming structure Chaucer employed in the writing of his Tales.

**Finding the rhythm**  Follow the rhythm of the verse (iambic pentameter), sounding or omitting the final 'e' syllable in the word as seems most appropriate. An 'e' before an 'h', for example, almost always disappears, as in the following:

> **Of Clytermystra, for hir(e) lecherie,**
>
> **That falsely mad(e) hir(e) housbond(e) for to die**

To sound the final 'e' on both examples of 'hire', as well as 'made' and 'housbonde' would be to add superfluous syllables. And in the case of this example:

> **Somme seyde wommen loven best richesse,**
>
> **Somme seyd(e) honour, somme seyde jolinesse –**

the best swing to the regular 10-syllabled line is achieved by sounding the 'e' (as a neutral vowel sound, like the 'u' in 'put', or the 'a' in 'about') in the word 'seyde' on two occasions, but not before 'honour'.

**Other points**  In words beginning with the letter 'y' (for example, 'ywet', 'yknowe') the 'y' is sounded as it would be in the modern 'party'. Many consonants now silent were pronounced - as in 'knight', 'wrong'. All the consonants would be given voice in words such as 'neigheboures' and 'knight' and the 'gh' would be sounded like the Scots 'ch' in 'loch'. The combination 'ow' (for example, 'seistow', 'yow') is pronounced as in 'how', and the 'ei' in 'seist' would be like the 'a' sound in 'pay'.

For more ideas of what the language might have sounded like, listen to the tapes of Chaucer published by Cambridge University Press and the 'Chaucer Man' (Trevor Eaton).

# WARM-UP ACTIVITIES

- Choose a long, self-contained section from the text: the first 34 lines of the Wife's Prologue are a useful example, since there is good reason for supposing she delivered these with scarcely a pause for breath! After a brief explanation of the content, if considered necessary, students work in pairs, speaking alternately, and changing over at each punctuation point. It should be possible to develop a fair turn of speed without losing the sense of the passage.
- Again in pairs, choose about 10 lines of text; as one of the pair maintains a steady

beat [^/^/^/^/^/] the partner does his or her best to fit the words to the rhythm.
- Choose a long self-contained unit from the text. Students walk round the room, speaking the script, and turning left or right at each punctuation mark. An alternative to this might be to use one 'speaker' representing the Wife, addressing four or five 'listeners', representing her audience. Each time the speaker reaches a punctuation mark he/she should look at a new listener, who should respond by looking alert and animated, being only allowed to sink back into apathy when she moves to the next one.
- A variation on the above activity could be developed using some part of the Wife's outbursts against husbands (see lines 235-322). One student could take the part of the hapless husband, facing one, or even three or four fierce 'wives', who take it in turns to deliver their complaints.

## GRAMMATICAL POINTS

**Emphatic negatives**  Whereas a person who stated that he 'wasn't going nowhere, not never' might be considered grammatically incorrect nowadays, Chaucer uses double or triple negatives quite often, to give a statement powerful added emphasis. One of the best known is in his description of the Knight in the General Prologue:

> **He never yet no vilenye ne sayde**
> **In al his life, unto no manner wight.**

Another occurs in the Wife of Bath's prologue:

> **... may they nat biquethe for no thing**
> **To noon of us hir vertuous living.**

In both cases the multiple negatives strengthen the force of what is being said.

**Word elision**  In modern written English words and phrases are often run together (elided) to represent the spoken form of those words: - 'didn't', 'can't', 'won't', 'I've', and so on. Chaucer uses short forms of words too, usually when a character is speaking, and most frequently when he is using 'tow' meaning thou (you). Examples include the following:

| | |
|---|---|
| **seistow** – you say | **wenestow** – do you intend |
| **hastow** – you have | **wostow why?** – do you know why? |

**The 'y' prefix**  The past tense of a verb (particularly when the verb is passive) sometimes has a 'y' before the rest of the verb:

| | |
|---|---|
| **yblessed moot he be** | he must be blessed |
| **yflattered and yplesed** | were flattered and pleased |
| **her joly whistle wel ywet** | her whistle had been well wet – i.e. she had had a great deal to drink |

**The 'possessive' form of nouns**  In modern English we indicate possession by means of an apostrophe: 'the hat of the man' becomes 'the man's hat'. Middle English had a particular formation that is still used in modern German. Where we now use an apostrophe followed by an 's', Chaucer uses the suffix 'es': 'the man's hat' becomes 'the mannes hat', the extra 'n' indicating that the word has two syllables.

# The Wife of Bath's contribution

Chaucer promises at the beginning of the Tales that he will describe all his pilgrims, telling the audience something of their status and their personality. He lists them in rough order of precedence, beginning with the Knight and his party (his son, the Squire, and their Yeoman servant). He continues with the group of religious characters who have status and importance (the Prioress, the Monk and the Friar), and then moves down through the social ranks, listing well-to-do middle class individuals and those with some wealth, followed by more lowly commoners. He ends his list with two unashamedly corrupt servants of the church, the Summoner and the Pardoner. This introduction, as fascinating and informative as many of the tales which follow, has come to be known as the 'General Prologue'. A short list of the pilgrims who feature in the complete work may be found on page 99.

The Wife of Bath appears amongst the people of substance and standing, after the Doctor of Physic and, ironically, immediately before the Parson, whose deep concern for the spiritual welfare of his parishoners contrasts oddly with the Wife's attitude to church-going and life in general. She likes to be noticed, dresses accordingly, and, above all, centres her life around the pursuit of men and the state of marriage.

Her creator offers the reader her character sketch without comment or undue emphasis, hinting at much that is left untold at this stage. It is with her introduction to her own tale that she blossoms most fully into life. Where the coyly modest Prioress has to be cajoled into speaking, the Wife cannot be silenced. Her own affairs and her life story take twice as long to tell as her actual Tale, and even the Tale itself is interrupted by her own views, and certainly reflects her own wishful thinking. The audience may like her or loathe her, but she cannot be ignored, and her exasperating and provocative views on marriage, men and mastery throw down a challenge taken up by many other pilgrims, most notably the Clerk, the Franklin and the Merchant. Chaucer does not necessarily agree with what his character says. Sometimes he invites the reader to find flaws in her belief in herself and her lifestyle. Her Prologue and Tale offer a variety of points of view, to be debated by her fellow travellers, as well as by the wider audience of Chaucer's readers.

- Working with a partner, pick out and list the factual details Chaucer gives us about the Wife in this description. Then discuss together what you think you can deduce about her character from these facts.
- Write your own description of a man or woman of today, using Chaucer's method of building up character from small details of dress, habit and appearance. You might write a description of someone similar to the Wife herself, identifying how she might dress, look and spend her time in the twentieth century.
- What is this woman doing on a pilgrimage at all? Chaucer invites us to ask this question about many of his pilgrims.

448 **somdel deef** a bit deaf [we learn why later]

**scathe** a pity

449 **hadde swich an haunt** had such skill

450 **Ypres and Gaunt** [Great cloth-making centres in Flanders. Weavers had considerable status and their skills were highly valued.]

452 **to the offringe** [At church services the congregation walked up to the altar to make their donations, strictly in order of social importance.]

453 **so wrooth was she** she was so furious

454 **out of alle charitee** out of temper

455 **hir coverchiefs** [These would be sizeable cloth head-dresses, draped over a frame made of wire, whalebone or dried grasses.]

459 **ful streite yteyd** [Stockings were held up with garters to avoid wrinkles – no elastic in those days. Red was a popular colour, but often reserved for people of high social status since it was an expensive dye.]

462 **at chirche dore** [Only the nobility were married in front of the altar; commoners met the priest at the door.]

464 **nedeth nat to speke as nowthe** there's no need to go into that [clearly a delicate subject]

466 **many a straunge strem** [Chaucer lists here the great centres of pilgrimage of the Christian world - Jerusalem, Cologne, Santiago de Compostela. Pilgrims travelled great distances in the fourteenth century, usually in large groups, not always exclusively for devout reasons.]

469 **koude muchel of wandringe by the weye** she knows a lot about travelling [but it's an ambiguous phrase: 'wandering by the way' suggests philandering too]

*The Wife of Bath as depicted in the Ellesmere manuscript. This was written and decorated in the fifteenth century, but reproduced the style of dress of the 1380s*

12

*The description of the Wife from the General Prologue*

A good Wif was ther of biside Bathe,
But she was somdel deef, and that was scathe.
Of clooth-making she hadde swich an haunt,
She passed hem of Ypres and of Gaunt.                     450
In al the parisshe wif ne was ther noon
That to the offringe bifore hire sholde goon;
And if ther dide, certeyn so wrooth was she,
That she was out of alle charitee.
Hir coverchiefs ful fine weren of ground;                 455
I dorste swere they weyeden ten pound
That on a Sonday weren upon hir heed.
Hir hosen weren of fyn scarlet reed,
Ful streite yteyd, and shoes ful moiste and newe.
Boold was hir face, and fair, and reed of hewe.           460
She was a worthy womman al hir live:
Housbondes at chirche dore she hadde five,
Withouten oother compaignye in youthe,—
But therof nedeth nat to speke as nowthe.
And thries hadde she been at Jerusalem;                   465
She hadde passed many a straunge strem;
At Rome she hadde been, and at Boloigne,
In Galice at Seint-Jame, and at Coloigne.
She koude muchel of wandringe by the weye.
Gat-tothed was she, soothly for to seye.                  470
Upon an amblere esily she sat,
Ywimpled wel, and on hir heed an hat
As brood as is a bokeler or a targe;
A foot-mantel aboute hir hipes large,
And on hir feet a paire of spores sharpe.                 475
In felaweshipe wel koude she laughe and carpe.
Of remedies of love she knew per chaunce,
For she koude of that art the olde daunce.

- *'Auctoritee'* comes from the scriptures and the teachings of learned men. The view of many rigid moralists within the church was that women were weak, sinful and, at best, a necessary evil. The Wife says that she has been told that she should only have married once, and mentions 'sharp words' spoken to her. What exactly are the criticisms she has received, and on what grounds? Discuss with a partner the circumstances in which these 'sharp words' might have taken place.
- What we already know from the description of the Wife suggests that she will not have taken such criticism kindly. Make a note of the way in which she handles her own defence.
- How does Chaucer make his verse read like informal speech?

| | | |
|---|---|---|
| 5 | **eterne on live** immortal | |
| 13 | **I ne sholde wedded be but ones** I should only be married once [Church authority questioned the legality of second marriages on Biblical evidence such as this.] | |
| 14 | **for the nones** appropriate in these circumstances | |
| 16 | **the Samaritan** [In St John 4, verse 6, Jesus offered the Samaritan 'living water' (spiritual purity) instead of | |

worldly pleasures. The Wife is deaf to the implication of the story, choosing to debate it her own way. See the note on Biblical references on page 00 for fuller details.]

24 **Yet herde I … diffinicioun** in all my life I have never heard any definition of this

26 **devine and glosen** guess and explain

27 **expres** explicitly

*The Wife leaps into her life story, prepared to challenge the 'auctoritee' of the church by speaking*
*from experience about the misery of marriage. Moral authority in the fourteenth century lay in the*
*hands of the Church and of those who spoke or wrote about the teachings of philosophers and*
*saints. It seems clear that she feels defensive about her many marriages and relishes this opportunity*
*to have her say. By allowing an illiterate commoner – and a woman at that – to challenge the*
*accepted standpoint Chaucer is offering a startling and quite controversial slant on life.*

'Experience, though noon auctoritee
Were in this world, is right ynogh for me
To speke of wo that is in mariage;
For, lordinges, sith I twelve yeer was of age,
Thonked be God that is eterne on live,                    5
Housbondes at chirche dore I have had five—
If I so ofte mighte have ywedded bee—
And alle were worthy men in hir degree.
But me was toold, certeyn, nat longe agoon is,
That sith that Crist ne wente nevere but onis          10
To wedding, in the Cane of Galilee,
That by the same ensample taughte he me
That I ne sholde wedded be but ones.
Herkne eek, lo, which a sharp word for the nones,
Biside a welle, Jhesus, God and man,                      15
Spak in repreeve of the Samaritan:
"Thou hast yhad five housbondes," quod he,
"And that ilke man that now hath thee
Is noght thyn housbonde," thus seyde he certeyn.
What that he mente therby, I kan nat seyn;              20
But that I axe, why that the fifthe man
Was noon housbonde to the Samaritan?
How manye mighte she have in mariage?
Yet herde I nevere tellen in myn age
Upon this nombre diffinicioun.                             25
Men may devine and glosen, up and doun,
But wel I woot, expres, withoute lie,
God bad us for to wexe and multiplie;
That gentil text kan I wel understonde.

- The Wife's method of arguing is forceful, if sometimes flawed. How does Chaucer reveal the forcefulness of her speaking voice in lines 30-61? Working with a partner, take turns to act out her argument, accompanying what you say by the sort of gestures she might have used.
- Consider how you might argue against the various points she makes on this page.
- Find out brief details about the Biblical characters Solomon, Lameth, Abraham and Jacob. What do all the Wife's Biblical 'team' have in common?
- In spite of the fact that the Wife said (line 3) that she would discuss 'the wo that is in mariage' there is considerable evidence here that she strongly favours marriage. What reasons does she seem to have for giving it such strong support?

| | | | | |
|---|---|---|---|---|
| 31 | **lete** leave | | 49 | **th'apostle** St Paul [Corinthians 1, verse 7] |
| 33 | **octogamie** marrying eight times | | 50 | **a Goddes half** in God's name |
| 37-8 | **As wolde God … so ofte as he!** I wish God would let me enjoy life with as many partners as he had! | | 52 | **Bet is to be wedded than to brinne** better to marry than burn [in Hell] |
| 41 | **as to my wit** as I believe | | 53-4 | **What rekketh me … and his bigamie?** why should I care if folk are scandalised by wicked Lameth and his bigamy? |
| 43 | **so wel was him on live** such a great life he had | | | |
| 46 | **I wol nat kepe me chaast in al** I certainly don't want to remain unmarried | | 56 | **as ferforth as I kan** as far as I can tell |
| | | | 59 | **in any manere age** at any time in the past |

*Not only does she attack criticism with defensive common-sense, the Wife also finds examples of*
*holy men in the Bible who had plenty of wives. She challenges her audience to find proof of any*
*occasion when God actually condemned marriage.*

Eek wel I woot, he seyde myn housbonde                     30
Sholde lete fader and mooder, and take to me.
But of no nombre mencion made he,
Of bigamie, or of octogamie;
Why sholde men thanne speke of it vileynie?
   Lo, heere, the wise king, daun Salomon;                 35
I trowe he hadde wives mo than oon.
As wolde God it were leveful unto me
To be refresshed half so ofte as he!
Which yifte of God hadde he for alle his wives!
No man hath swich that in this world alive is.             40
God woot, this noble king, as to my wit,
The firste night had many a mirie fit
With ech of hem, so wel was him on live.
Yblessed be God that I have wedded five!
Welcome the sixte, whan that evere he shal.                45
For sothe, I wol nat kepe me chaast in al.
Whan myn housbonde is fro the world ygon,
Som Cristen man shal wedde me anon,
For thanne, th'apostle seith that I am free
To wedde, a Goddes half, where it liketh me.               50
He seith that to be wedded is no sinne;
Bet is to be wedded than to brinne.
What rekketh me, thogh folk seye vileynie
Of shrewed Lameth and his bigamie?
I woot wel Abraham was an hooly man,                       55
And Jacob eek, as ferforth as I kan;
And ech of hem badde wives mo than two,
And many another holy man also.
Wher can ye seye, in any manere age,
That hye God defended mariage                              60
By expres word? I pray yow, telleth me.
Or where comanded he virginitee?

- Do you consider the Wife argues her case for marriage well here? What debating techniques does she use, and how persuasively?
- How might some of her fellow pilgrims have reacted to the things she says? Consider, for example, the fastidious, tender-hearted Prioress, the scholarly and book-loving Clerk of Oxford, the Friar, who clearly admires pretty girls although he is a churchman, or the Knight, a model of chivalrous behaviour. You might choose to make your ideas the basis for classroom drama, or for a piece of creative writing.
- Discuss with a partner whether or not you think Chaucer agreed with the Wife's point of view, justifying your answer by using evidence from the text.

| | | | |
|---|---|---|---|
| 63 | **it is no drede** no two ways about it | 83-4 | **yaf me leve of indulgence; so nis it no repreve** gave me permission to live less strictly; so there is no need to disapprove of me at all [double negative gives extra emphasis] |
| 65 | **precept therof hadde he noon** he had no authority from God for his words | | |
| 70 | **dampned** condemned | | |
| 74 | **yaf noon heeste** gave no order | 85 | **make** mate, husband |
| 75-6 | **The dart is ... best lat see** the prize for achieving a life of perfect chastity has been set up in the Bible; let the rest of us stand back and see who can win it | 86 | **excepcion of bigamie** complaints that I am bigamous |
| | | 87 | **al were it** although it might be |
| | | 88 | **for peril is** for it's dangerous |
| 77-8 | **But this word ... of his might** the challenge of virginity is not taken up by everyone, only by those God has chosen through his power | 89 | **fyr and tow t'assemble** to put flame and flax together |
| | | 91 | **This is al and som** this is the long and the short of it |
| 82 | **al nis but** this is nothing more than | | |

*The Wife admits that to be a virgin is a fine thing, admired by Biblical authorities and recommended as the perfect state by God. But, she protests, it doesn't suit everyone, nor was it ever enforced as a commandment. After all, she argues, if everyone lived as a virgin, where would the next generation come from?*

I woot as wel as ye, it is no drede,
Th'apostel, whan he speketh of maidenhede,
He seyde that precept therof hadde he noon.            65
Men may conseille a womman to been oon,
But conseilling is no comandement.
He putte it in oure owene juggement;
For hadde God comanded maidenhede,
Thanne hadde he dampned wedding with the dede.        70
And certes, if ther were no seed ysowe,
Virginitee, thanne wherof sholde it growe?
Poul dorste nat comanden, atte leeste,
A thing of which his maister yaf noon heeste.
The dart is set up for virginitee:                    75
Cacche whoso may, who renneth best lat see.
   But this word is nat taken of every wight,
But ther as God lust give it of his might.
I woot wel that th'apostel was a maide;
But nathelees, thogh that he wroot and saide          80
He wolde that every wight were swich as he,
Al nis but conseil to virginitee.
And for to been a wyf he yaf me leve
Of indulgence; so nis it no repreve
To wedde me, if that my make die,                     85
Withouten excepcion of bigamie.
Al were it good no womman for to touche,—
He mente as in his bed or in his couche;
For peril is bothe fyr and tow t'assemble:
Ye knowe what this ensample may resemble.             90
This is al and som, he heeld virgintee
Moore parfit than wedding in freletee.

- The Wife makes three quite separate points in her own defence in lines 99-128. What are they? Which seems the most convincing to you?
- Just look back and remind yourself what the Wife was being criticised for in the first place. What has happened to her argument?
- How do you think her tone would differ from line 115 onwards?

95   **I graunte ... I have noon envie** I am quite happy with this, I don't envy them this status

96   **bigamie** marrying more than once [in this context]

101   **somme been of tree** some are made of wood

106   **continence eek with devocion** self-restraint linked with devout behaviour

107   **that of perfeccion is welle** who is the source of all perfection

110   **his foore** his footsteps

119   **Glose whoso wole ... up and doun** try to interpret differently if you like, argue this way and that

121   **oure bothe thinges smale** our various male and female bits and pieces

123   **say ye no?** can you deny that I am right?

127-8   **for office, and for ese of engendrure** for passing water and also for enjoying procreation

*The Virgin and Child portrayed in the Wilton Diptych painted in 1395: 'Virginitee is greet perfeccion, And continence eek with devocion'*

*The Wife begins to build up the case for her own more physical lifestyle.*

Freletee clepe I, but if that he and she
Wolde leden al hir lyf in chastitee.
   I graunte it wel, I have noon envie,         95
Thogh maidenhede preferre bigamie.
It liketh hem to be clene, body and goost;
Of myn estaat I nil nat make no boost.
For wel ye knowe, a lord in his houshold,
He nath nat every vessel al of gold;         100
Somme been of tree, and doon hir lord servise.
God clepeth folk to hym in sondry wise,
And everich hath of God a propre yifte,
Som this, som that, as him liketh shifte.
   Virginitee is greet perfeccion,         105
And continence eek with devocion,
But Crist, that of perfeccion is welle,
Bad nat every wight he sholde go selle
Al that he hadde, and give it to the poore
And in swich wise folwe him and his foore.         110
He spak to hem that wolde live parfitly;
And lordinges, by youre leve, that am nat I.
I wol bistowe the flour of al myn age
In the actes and in fruit of mariage.
   Telle me also, to what conclusion         115
Were membres maad of generacion,
And of so parfit wys a wight ywroght?
Trusteth right wel, they were nat maad for noght.
Glose whoso wole, and seye bothe up and doun,
That they were maked for purgacioun         120
Of urine, and oure bothe thinges smale
Were eek to knowe a femele from a male,
And for noon oother cause,—say ye no?
The experience woot wel it is noght so.
So that the clerkes be nat with me wrothe,         125
I sey this, that they maked ben for bothe,
This is to seye, for office, and for ese
Of engendrure, ther we nat God displese.

In the first 162 lines the Wife challenges some of the fundamental and powerful arguments used by church and scholarship to dictate the roles of men and women, workers and scholars in fourteenth century England. She fights for all women, in a society dominated by men; but she also champions common sense and experience, attacking strict, unworldly ideals of perfection, virginity and abstinence presented as the ideal life by preachers and scholars.

Chaucer invites us to take part in the debate, offering opportunities to find flaws in her arguments as well as in the views she attacks. Remember the author's view is not necessarily that of his creation, though he might well sympathise. Chaucer was a scholar, passionately interested in literature and ideas. He was also a great observer of the life going on around him. He lived in a period of social change, when the right of the Catholic Church to dictate how people should live was frequently challenged.

• Does the Wife make a good case for marriage in these first 162 lines? Would her views of the rights of wives, and the way she expresses them, make her a pleasant marriage partner? (Look particularly at lines 154-5.) And what do you think of her way of constructing her case? Is she logical? Does she twist the facts? What does she mean here by 'experience'? You might consider discussing these points with a partner; running a classroom debate on 'Chastity versus marriage' or 'Wifeliness is next to Godliness'; or 'hot seating' the Wife – making her defend her position against other members of the class acting as churchmen or scholars.

At the back of this book you will find summaries of the Biblical passages she uses in this first section of prologue, together with some factual information about women in the fourteenth century, and the role of the church, all of which might be helpful.

| | | | |
|---|---|---|---|
| 132, 136, 149 | sely instrument, harneys and instrument [all words used to denote sexual organs] | 148 | I nam nat precius I am not over-genteel or fastidious |
| 133 | Thanne were they maad upon a creature they were given to mankind for these reasons | 154-5 | An housbonde I wol have ... and my thral I will have a husband, no one shall stop me and he shall pay me my rightful dues and be my slave |
| 138 | Thanne sholde men take of chastitee no cure if this were so men would not value chastity | 162 | Al this sentence me liketh every deel I approve of this statement entirely |
| 142 | I nil envye no virginitee I don't begrudge anyone else being a virgin | | |

*The Wife expands upon points made earlier, introducing a new element — the nature of marriage
itself, and what husbands and wives owe to one another. Those who do marry are like humble
barley bread, whereas virgins are pure wheat loaves, and both have their uses.*

Why sholde men elles in hir bookes sette
That man shal yelde to his wyf hire dette?       130
Now wherwith sholde he make his paiement,
If he ne used his sely instrument?
Thanne were they maad upon a creature
To purge urine, and eek for engendrure.
    But I seye noght that every wight is holde,       135
That hath swich harneys as I to yow tolde,
To goon and usen hem in engendrure.
Thanne sholde men take of chastitee no cure.
Crist was a maide, and shapen as a man,
And many a seint, sith that the world bigan;       140
Yet lived they evere in parfit chastitee.
I nil envye no virginitee.
Lat hem he breed of pured whete-seed,
And lat us wives hoten barly-breed;
And yet with barly-breed, Mark telle kan,       145
Oure Lord Jhesu refresshed many a man.
In swich estaat as God hath cleped us
I wol persevere; I nam nat precius.
In wyfhod I wol use myn instrument
As frely as my Makere hath it sent.       150
If I be daungerous, God yeve me sorwe!
Myn housbonde shal it have bothe eve and morwe,
Whan that him list come forth and paye his dette.
An housbonde I wol have, I wol nat lette,
Which shal be bothe my dettour and my thral,       155
And have his tribulacion withal
Upon his flessh, whil that I am his wyf.
I have the power duringe al my lyf
Upon his propre body, and noght he.
Right thus the Apostel tolde it unto me;       160
And bad oure housbondes for to love us weel.
Al this sentence me liketh every deel.'

Chaucer's Pardoner is not a pleasant man. He makes a fat profit from the sale of 'pardons', brought back from Rome, or simply written when required. These pieces of paper could be bought as a sign of the remorse a sinner felt for his or her sins. By the fourteenth century many people bought pardons as insurance policies, after which they happily continued to live sinful lives. He also allows religious people to see and worship his collection of 'relics', which he carries with him – provided they pay for the privilege. Chaucer shows contempt for these in the General Prologue, by calling his saints' relics 'pigges bones', and by telling us that what the Pardoner calls part of the Virgin Mary's veil is really a scrap of old pillow case. It is hard to believe his statement that he is to be married, for Chaucer elsewhere strongly implies that he was a eunuch – both physically and spiritually deficient – so this is possibly an empty boast. He is clearly an enthusiastic drinker, for Chaucer mentions his love of strong ale when he tells his own story. The General Prologue suggests he fancies himself as a fashionable and dashing figure, and the reference in line 187 to 'us yonge men' reminds us of this.

• The interruption by the Pardoner brings about a natural break in the Wife's words. What reasons might Chaucer have had for introducing it? Amongst other things think about what the conversation on this page reveals of the Wife's personality.

| | | | |
|---|---|---|---|
| 164 | **dame** my lady [the Pardoner may be speaking ironically] | | whether you yourself wish to drink from the barrel that I break open - be very careful of it, before you get too close |
| 165 | **in this cas** on this subject | | |
| 167 | **bye it on my flessh so deere** pay so highly for such misery | 180 | **nil be war** will not be warned |
| 168 | **levere wedde no wyf to-yeere** rather marry no wife this year | 182-3 | **The same wordes ... take it there** [Refers to the Greek scholar, astrologer and geographer, Ptolemy – in the early middle ages the works of such 'pagan' writers were banned by the church, to be rediscovered later by western medieval scholars, since they had been preserved and translated by the Arabs. The title 'Almageste' comes from the Arabic.] |
| 170-1 | **thou shalt drinken ... wors than ale** you're going to hear my side of the story [*literally:* you'll drink from a different barrel, that will taste worse than your beer, before I've finished] | | |
| 174 | **expert in al myn age** having years of experience | | |
| 176-8 | **Than maystow chese ... to ny approche** then you may choose | 187 | **praktike** habits, way of behaving |

*The Wife is interrupted by the Pardoner, who compliments her preaching skills, but claims she has made marriage sound so unattractive that he has decided not to take a wife himself. Don't make up your mind too quickly, says the Wife, I have a great deal more to tell you. With great politeness the Pardoner begs her to continue.*

Up stirte the Pardoner, and that anon:
'Now, dame,' quod he, 'by God and by Seint John!
Ye been a noble prechour in this cas.                     165
I was aboute to wedde a wyf; allas,
What sholde I bye it on my flessh so deere?
Yet hadde I levere wedde no wyf to-yeere!'
    'Abide!' quod she, 'my tale is nat bigonne.
Nay, thou shalt drinken of another tonne,                 170
Er that I go, shal savoure wors than ale.
And whan that I have toold thee forth my tale
Of tribulacion in mariage,
Of which I am expert in al myn age—
This is to seyn, myself have been the whippe—            175
Than maystow chese wheither thou wolt sippe
Of thilke tonne that I shal abroche.
Be war of it, er thou to ny approche;
For I shal telle ensamples mo than ten.
"Whoso that nil be war by othere men,                    180
By him shul othere men corrected be."
The same wordes writeth Ptholomee;
Rede in his Almageste, and take it there.'
    'Dame, I wolde praye yow, if youre wil it were,'
Seyde this Pardoner, 'as ye bigan,                       185
Telle forth youre tale, spareth for no man,
And teche us yonge men of youre praktike.'
    'Gladly,' quod she, 'sith it may yow like;
But that I praye to al this compaignie,
If that I speke after my fantasie,                       190
As taketh not agrief of that I seye;
For myn entente is nat but for to pleye.
Now, sire, now wol I telle forth my tale.

- The Wife says 'myn entente is nat but for to pleye'. When you have read on to the end of the prologue, decide why Chaucer inserted this statement. Does it affect your opinion of what the Wife has to say in the account which follows?
- On the evidence so far, what is likely to make her think that three husbands were good and two bad? What is suggested about her views on sex and power?
- A day in the life of this woman's husband was clearly unpleasant. Note carefully what she says about her behaviour (lines 199-223), and, using this as your basis, present some classroom improvisations; write a page from a diary (his or hers); or write a letter to the 'problem page' of a magazine.
- Do you agree with her statement in lines 209-10? What does it suggest about the things women consider important?

| | |
|---|---|
| **198** | **unnethe** hardly or scarcely |
| **198-200** | **Unnethe ... pardee** [The Wife is being coy here, referring to the fact that her old husbands were worn out trying to satisfy her sexually.] |
| **203** | **I tolde of it no stoor** I was not concerned [about their distress] |
| **205-6** | **Me neded nat ... reverence** there was no longer any need for me to try to win their love, or behave respectfully towards them |
| **208** | **ne tolde no deyntee of hir love** did not value their love |
| **209** | **evere in oon** all the while |

| | |
|---|---|
| **213-4** | **What sholde I ... and myn ese?** Why should I bother to please them, unless it were for my own profit and comfort? |
| **216** | **weilawey!** oh, woe is me! |
| **217-8** | **The bacon ... Dunmowe** [A reference to the custom still observed in Dunmow, Essex – a married couple who could prove they had not quarrelled during the year would be awarded a 'flitch' or a side of bacon.] |
| **220** | **fawe** delighted |

*Instead of beginning her Tale, the Wife continues to discuss her own life. She says she had three good husbands – old, rich men – and two bad ones. She describes married life with the three 'good' men.*

As evere moote I drinken wyn or ale,
I shal seye sooth, tho housbondes that I hadde,          195
As thre of hem were goode, and two were badde.
The thre were goode men, and riche, and olde;
Unnethe mighte they the statut holde
In which that they were bounden unto me.
Ye woot wel what I meene of this, pardee.               200
As help me God, I laughe whan I thinke
How pitously a-night I made hem swinke!
And, by my fey, I tolde of it no stoor.
They had me yeven hir lond and hir tresoor;
Me neded nat do lenger diligence                        205
To winne hir love, or doon hem reverence.
They loved me so wel, by God above,
That I ne tolde no deyntee of hir love.
A wys womman wol bisie hire evere in oon
To gete hir love, ye, ther as she hath noon.            210
But sith I hadde hem hoolly in myn hond,
And sith they hadde me yeven al hir lond,
What sholde I taken keep hem for to plese,
But it were for my profit and myn ese?
I sette hem so a-werke, by my fey,                      215
That many a night they songen "weilawey!"
The bacon was nat fet for hem, I trowe,
That som men han in Essex at Dunmowe.
I governed hem so wel, after my lawe,
That ech of hem ful blisful was and fawe                220
To bringe me gaye thinges fro the faire.
They were ful glad whan I spak to hem faire;
For, God it woot, I chidde hem spitously.

- In the long section in lines 235-378 Chaucer gives the Wife a list of actions and statements that illuminate traditional and stereotypical areas of disagreement between men and women. Every stand-up comedian from the fourteenth century onwards has probably used some of this material in his or her routine. Why does Chaucer include it here? At the end of the section (line 382) the Wife turns to her audience of pilgrims, telling them that her poor old husbands never said any of these things at all, she merely pretended that they said them. So what has Chaucer gained by putting it all in? Discuss this with a partner first, and then in a larger group. Consider two things: how this passage adds to our understanding of the Wife herself; and also what it adds to the whole question of male/female relationships that Chaucer scrutinises in this Prologue and Tale.
- Line 246 offers the opportunity for some character acting in pairs. The husband comes home 'as drunk as a mouse' (why a mouse? does this give an idea of his personality? or did mice often fall into beer vats?) and begins to 'preach' to his wife. Presumably she has a great deal to say in return. With a partner, work on a piece of similar dialogue between a modern man and wife — do people still argue about the same issues as those in Chaucer's text?

| | |
|---|---|
| 224 | **hou I baar me proprely** how cleverly I handled things |
| 226 | **shulde** should |
| | **bere hem wrong on honde** trick them, deceive them |
| 230 | **hem misavise** get themselves into trouble |
| 231-4 | **A wys wyf shal ... Of hir assent** [A well-known story of the time concerned a talking bird, a chough ('cow'), which told its master when his wife entertained her lover in her husband's absence. She said the bird was mad, but he refused to believe her. The next night the wife and her maid made noises like a thunderstorm over the bird's cage. On hearing the bird complain of the terrible storm, the man decided that the bird had lost its senses, and dismissed the tale of the visiting lover.] |

| | |
|---|---|
| 235 | **Sire olde kaynard, is this thyn array?** so, master, you old fool, is this the way you carry on? |
| 236 | **so gay** so well-dressed |
| 238 | **no thrifty clooth** not a thing to wear |
| 239 | **dostow** what do you do? |
| 240 | **artow** are you? |
| 241 | **rowne** whisper |
| | *Benedicite!* God bless us! |
| 242 | **lat thy japes be** stop this messing about |
| 244 | **withouten gilt** quite innocently |
| 247 | **with ivel preef** bad luck to you |
| 249 | **costage** expense |
| 250 | **heigh parage** noble birth |
| 254 | **holour** lecher |

*The Wife offers advice to all women on how to 'keep men under control'. She suggests leaping into the attack first, and accusing them of unacceptable behaviour before they have the opportunity to begin making their own criticisms.*

Now herkneth hou I baar me proprely,
Ye wise wives, that kan understonde.                        225
Thus shulde ye speke and bere hem wrong on honde;
For half so boldely kan ther no man
Swere and lyen, as a womman kan.
I sey nat this by wives that been wise,
But if it be whan they hem misavise.                        230
A wys wyf shal, if that she kan hir good,
Bere him on honde that the cow is wood,
And take witnesse of hir owene maide
Of hir assent; but herkneth how I saide:
    "Sire olde kaynard, is this thyn array?             235
Why is my neighebores wyf so gay?
She is honoured over al ther she gooth;
I sitte at hoom, I have no thrifty clooth.
What dostow at my neighebores hous?
Is she so fair? artow so amorous?                          240
What rowne ye with oure maide? *Benedicite!*
Sire olde lecchour, lat thy japes be.
And if I have a gossib or a freend,
Withouten gilt, thou chidest as a feend,
If that I walke or pleye unto his hous.                    245
Thou comest hoom as dronken as a mous,
And prechest on thy bench, with ivel preef!
Thou seist to me it is a greet meschief
To wedde a povre womman, for costage;
And if that she be riche, of heigh parage,               250
Thanne seistow that it is a tormentrie
To soffre hire pride and hire malencolie.
And if that she be fair, thou verray knave,
Thou seist that every holour wol hire have;
She may no while in chastitee abide,                       255
That is assailled upon ech a side.

29

- One of Chaucer's other pilgrims (the Merchant) tells a tale about a man who has very precise specifications by which to choose his ideal bride. Using the information on this page and the preceding one, create an advertisement for the ideal wife. Alternatively, write your own specification for an ideal partner of either sex, and include, as Chaucer does, both those things that would be attractive, and also those faults or features you would not wish to find.
- The man supposedly speaking in this passage likens some women to spaniels and others to grey geese. What particular qualities of each of these creatures is he considering? Write a description of either a man or a woman in which you liken him or her to one or several creatures, making clear where the likeness appears.

    Alternatively, try your hand at producing a cartoon likeness of one of the characters mentioned by Chaucer on this page.

| | | | |
|---|---|---|---|
| 259 | **for she kan** because she knows how to | 273 | **lorel** wretch or miserable toad [an insulting word] |
| 260 | **daliaunce** flirtation | 275 | **entendeth unto** hopes to reach |
| 261 | **hir handes and hir armes smale** slender hands and arms [signs of great beauty in the 1300s] | 276-7 | **With wilde ... be tobroke!** with wild thunder claps and flashing lightning may your scraggy old neck be broken [The Wife seems to be working herself into a frenzy.] |
| 263-4 | **Thou seist men ... been overal** men cannot defend a wife's virtue [*literally:* a castle wall] for ever – if it is under constant attack it will finally be taken | 278-80 | **Thow seist ... owene hous** [The Wife is here quoting from St Jerome's adaptation of words from the Book of Proverbs 27, verse 12.] |
| 265 | **foul** ugly | 281 | **What eyleth ... chide?** What's wrong with an old man that he complains so much? |
| 266 | **coveiteth** fancies | | |
| 267 | **him** [not just one man: all of them] | 283 | **fast** safely married |
| 269-70 | **Ne noon so grey ... withoute make** there's no goose so grey [unattractive] on the lake, so you say, that she can't find a partner somewhere | 284 | **Wel may ... of a shrewe!** that's the sort of thing a misery like you would say |
| 271-2 | **And seist ... his thankes, helde** it's difficult to keep under control something that no man would willingly keep possession of | | |

*The Wife presents a catalogue of the reasons men have for marrying, mingled with the reasons men
have to complain about their wives. Lack of sexual restraint figures largely in this list.*

---

Thou seist som folk desiren us for richesse,
Somme for oure shap, and somme for oure fairnesse,
And som for she kan outher singe or daunce,
And som for gentillesse and daliaunce;                                    260
Som for hir handes and hir armes smale:
Thus goth al to the devel, by thy tale.
Thou seist men may nat kepe a castel wal,
It may so longe assailled been overal.

And if that she be foul, thou seist that she             265
Coveiteth every man that she may se,
For as a spaynel she wol on him lepe,
Til that she finde som man hire to chepe.
Ne noon so grey goos gooth ther in the lake
As, sëistow, wol been withoute make.                     270
And seist it is an hard thing for to welde
A thing that no man wole, his thankes, helde.
Thus seistow, lorel, whan thow goost to bedde;
And that no wys man nedeth for to wedde,
Ne no man that entendeth unto hevene.                    275
With wilde thonder-dint and firy levene
Moote thy welked nekke be tobroke!

Thow seist that dropping houses, and eek smoke,
And chiding wives maken men to flee
Out of hir owene hous; a, *benedicitee!*                 280
What eyleth swich an old man for to chide?

Thow seist we wives wol oure vices hide
Til we be fast, and thanne we wol hem shewe—
Wel may that be a proverbe of a shrewe!

Chaucer's source for the list of complaints in lines 235-315 is St Jerome's treatise condemning Jovinian's support of marriage, which itself is derived from the writings of the philosopher, Theophrastus (see note on line 671). Scholarly material and domestic trivialities are skilfully amalgamated, here and elsewhere.

- There are a number of complaints made in these lines both about the husband's behaviour and about the wife's. Do you consider any, or all, of them to be justified in any way? Although it has already been mentioned that she finally says the old husbands never said any of these things, are things mentioned here which seem likely to be a true commentary on the Wife's married life?
- What suggests to you from both the subject matter and the style of this page that the Wife is growing increasingly angry as she recalls life with her 'good' husbands?
- Is it possible to discern from what you have read so far the qualities of life the Wife values most? What would her modern equivalent be like? After discussion, write a magazine article along the lines of 'My perfect life – an interview with the Wife of Bath'.

286 **They been assayed ...stoundes** they can be tested/tried out on various occasions.

287 **Bacins, lavours ...** bowls, washbasins

288 **housbondrie** houseware

295 **but thou ... upon my face** unless you gaze lovingly at my face all the time

298 **make me fressh and gay** buy me fine new clothes to wear

299 **norice** nurse

300 **chamberere** chambermaid

301 **fadres folk and his allies** father's folk and relations

304 **crispe heer** curly hair

305 **squiereth me** keeps me company wherever I go

307 **I wol him noght** I wouldn't have him [but she does!]

308 **with sorwe** curse you

309 **cheste** sturdy, well-padlocked box

311 **wenestow** are you trying to

312-5 **Now by that lord ... maugree thine yen** I now swear by St James of Compostela you shall not have both my body and my possessions under your control. You'll have to give up one of the two, damn your eyes.

316 **helpith it** good does it do

317 **I trowe thou woldest** I think you'd like to

**chiste** chest

*'Why hidestow, with sorwe,*
*The keyes of thy cheste awey fro me?'*

*We are told the angry husband says all other household stock and animals can be tried out before buying, but no-one can test out a wife before marriage. He says she is angry if he fails to speak graciously to her, her family, friends and servant. He suspects (apparently falsely) her fondness for Jankin, the fair-haired apprentice. To her fury, her husband will not relinquish the keys to the money chest.*

Thou seist that oxen, asses, hors, and houndes,                285
They been assayed at diverse stoundes;
Bacins, lavours, er that men hem bye,
Spoones and stooles, and al swich housbondrie,
And so been pottes, clothes, and array;
But folk of wives maken noon assay,                            290
Til they be wedded; olde dotard shrewe!
And thanne, seistow, we wol oure vices shewe.
    Thou seist also that it displeseth me
But if that thou wolt preyse my beautee,
And but thou poure alwey upon my face,                         295
And clepe me 'faire dame' in every place.
And but thou make a feeste on thilke day
That I was born, and make me fressh and gay;
And but thou do to my norice honour,
And to my chamberere withinne my bour,                         300
And to my fadres folk and his allies—
Thou seistow, olde barel-ful of lies!
    And yet of oure apprentice Janekin,
For his crispe heer, shininge as gold so fyn,
And for he squiereth me bothe up and doun,                     305
Yet hastow caught a fals suspecioun.
I wol him noght, thogh thou were deed tomorwe!
    But tel me this: why hidestow, with sorwe,
The keyes of thy cheste awey fro me?
It is my good as wel as thyn, pardee!                          310
What, wenestow make an idiot of oure dame?
Now by that lord that called is Seint Jame,
Thou shalt nat bothe, thogh that thou were wood,
Be maister of my body and of my good;
That oon thou shalt forgo, maugree thine yen.                  315
What helpith it of me to enquere or spyen?
I trowe thou woldest loke me in thy chiste!

• In line 322 the Wife asserts that women need to be given their freedom. Freedom to do what? There have been a number of hints and some direct statements already of the sort of behaviour she is thinking of here. How strongly do the statements she makes on this page seem to contradict her declarations of virtue elsewhere? Find examples of her claims to virtue. Do you approve of her moral standpoint? Does Chaucer?

319    **Taak youre ... leve no talis** enjoy yourself, I will not believe any gossip about you

322    **we wol ben at oure large** we wish to have total freedom

324    **astrologien** astrologer

       **Daun Ptholome** [Ptolemy, whose book on astronomy , the 'Almageste', was much respected in the fourteenth century – see note to lines 182-3].

326-30    **Of alle men ... that othere folkes fare?** the wisest man is he who never bothers who else might own all the riches of the world. In other words, if you have sufficient for yourself, why make a fuss about what other folk might be enjoying?

332    **queynte** a woman's sexual parts

333-6    **He is to greet ... nat pleyne thee** anyone who complains if another man borrows his lantern to light a candle is far too much of a miser. By God it doesn't interfere with the amount of light he enjoys himself. You have as much as you want [to her old husband], so stop moaning.

339    **peril of** a danger to

341    **the Apostles name** [refers to St Paul's first letter to St Timothy 2 verse 9]

344    **tressed heer and gay perree** braided hair and fine gems

346-7    **After thy text ... as a gnat** I don't care a fly for your Biblical text, nor for the way you interpret it

*The Wife imagines a happy state in which she is given complete freedom to do whatever she wishes·*
*by a trusting husband. Women can't bear to be restrained, she says. The philosopher Ptolemy said*
*that miserable people always envy what others possess. After all, if her old husband is able to enjoy*
*sex with her whenever he wants it, why should he begrudge others her favours, she asks. She has no*
*patience with his complaint that fine clothes are an indication of a woman's lack of chastity and*
*self-control.*

Thou sholdest seye, 'Wyf, go wher thee liste;
Taak youre disport, I wol nat leve no talis.
I knowe yow for a trewe wyf, dame Alis.'                    320
We love no man that taketh kep or charge
Wher that we goon; we wol ben at oure large.
  Of alle men yblessed moot he be,
The wise astrologien, Daun Ptholome,
That seith this proverbe in his Almageste:                  325
'Of alle men his wisdom is the hyeste
That rekketh nevere who hath the world in honde.'
By this proverbe thou shalt understonde,
Have thou ynogh, what thar thee recche or care
How mirily that othere folkes fare?                         330
For, certeyn, olde dotard, by youre leve,
Ye shul have queynte right ynogh at eve.
He is to greet a nigard that wolde werne
A man to lighte a candle at his lanterne;
He shal have never the lasse light, pardee.                 335
Have thou ynogh, thee thar nat pleyne thee.
  Thou seist also, that if we make us gay
With clothing, and with precious array,
That it is peril of oure chastitee;
And yet, with sorwe! thou most enforce thee,                340
And seye thise wordes in the Apostles name:
'In habit maad with chastitee and shame
Ye wommen shul apparaille yow,' quod he,
'And noght in tressed heer and gay perree,
As perles, ne with gold, ne clothes riche.'                 345
After thy text, ne after thy rubriche,
I wol nat wirche as muchel as a gnat.

- Presumably the list of sayings that the Wife reels off in these lines would have been familiar to her audience: 'Give a woman a new dress and she'll be off on the tiles just like any cat,' and so on. Make a list of the sayings she mentions here, then, with a partner, make up a few of your own – perhaps about husbands for a change.

353-4   **But forth ... a-caterwawed** but off she'll go before daybreak, to show her fine clothes and to have a good time

356   **my borel** ['Borel' was actually rather rough coarse cloth. The Wife may be speaking sarcastically; she has already referred to the meanness of husbands who don't provide new clothes readily.]

358-60   **Argus with his hundred yen** [Argus was a mythical hundred-eyed creature. The Wife is saying that even if this creature were her guardian, she would still break free, if she wished.]

361   **make his berd** outwit him

362   **so moot I thee!** I can tell you! or I promise you!

364   **the ferthe** the fourth

367   **yrekened is** is reckoned to be

368-370 **Been ther none ... be oon of tho?** are there no other comparisons that you could use for your parables? Do you have to keep comparing dreadful things to poor innocent wives?

371   **thou liknest** you compare

374   **brenneth** burns

376-7   **right as wormes ... hire housbonde** just as insects can destroy a tree, so a woman can destroy her husband

*'And if the cattes skin be slik and gay,*
*She wol nat dwelle in house half a day.'*

*Women are supposedly like cats, showing off and enjoying themselves only when they look sleek and fine. The Wife tells her old husbands they spy on her in vain – she will never be restrained against her will. She says the old men utter all sorts of curses and complaints against wives – at least that is how she tells them they behaved when they were drunk.*

Thou seydest this, that I was lyk a cat;
For whoso wolde senge a cattes skin,
Thanne wolde the cat wel dwellen in is in;          350
And if the cattes skin be slik and gay,
She wol nat dwelle in house half a day,
But forth she wole, er any day be dawed,
To shewe hir skin, and goon a-caterwawed.
This is to seye, if I be gay, sire shrewe,          355
I wol renne out, my borel for to shewe.
    Sire olde fool, what helpeth thee to spyen?
Thogh thou preye Argus with his hundred yen
To be my warde-cors, as he kan best,
In feith, he shal nat kepe me but me lest;          360
Yet koude I make his berd, so moot I thee!
    Thou seydest eek that ther been thinges thre,
The whiche thinges troublen al this erthe,
And that no wight may endure the ferthe.
O leeve sire shrewe, Jhesu shorte thy lyf!          365
Yet prechestow and seist an hateful wyf
Yrekened is for oon of thise meschances.
Been ther none othere maner resemblances
That ye may likne youre parables to,
But if a sely wyf be oon of tho?                    370
    Thou liknest eek wommenes love to helle,
To bareyne lond, ther water may nat dwelle.
Thou liknest it also to wilde fyr;
The moore it brenneth, the moore it hath desir
To consume every thing that brent wole be.         375
Thou seyest, right as wormes shende a tree,
Right so a wyf destroyeth hire housbonde;
This knowe they that been to wives bonde."

37

- The mood of the narration changes at line 379, as the Wife turns to address the 'lordinges' – the other pilgrims. When you have read up to line 450, consider how the Wife's tone or attitude has changed. How does she speak lines 379-83? And how might her fellow-pilgrims react to her?
- What proof do you find on this page that the Wife enjoys boasting about her dominating behaviour? Note the way she speaks, and the statements she makes in lines 379-407 which suggest enjoyment and self-justification. Compare your list with a partner.
- The Wife seems to suggest that all women will behave as she does because it is their nature. How seriously should the reader take such statements?

| | |
|---|---|
| 380-1 | **Baar I stifly ... in hir dronkenesse** thus did I boldly lie and deceive my old husbands, telling them this was the sort of thing they said to me when they were drunk |
| 385 | **giltelees** guiltless |
| | **by Goddes sweete pine!** by the Lord's blessed agony |
| 387-8 | **I koude pleyne ... hadde I been spilt** I could make complaints even if I was the guilty one myself; otherwise my misdoings would often have been discovered |
| 388-9 | **Whoso that first ... oure werre ystint** whoever gets to the mill first, grinds first [and so, by making sure she gets her word in first, the Wife prevents fiercer arguments] |
| 392 | **agilte** guilty |
| 393 | **beren hem on honde** accuse them [of having affairs] |
| 394 | **Whan that for sik unnethes mighte they stonde** when they were almost too ill to stand |

| | |
|---|---|
| 395 | **tikled I his herte** I pleased and flattered him [she makes no distinction between the three 'good husbands'] |
| 396 | **wende** believed |
| | **so greet chiertee** such a great fondness |
| 398 | **dighte** had sex with |
| 399 | **under that colour** using this pretence |
| 403-6 | **And thus ... murmur or grucching** and so I certainly boast of one thing: ultimately I got the better of my husband in every way, through some method – trickery, forcefulness, or perhaps continual moaning or nagging |
| 407 | **Namely** most particularly |
| 411 | **maad his raunson** paid his forfeit |
| 412 | **suffre him do his nicetee** let him have his way with me |

*Jankin and her niece were accomplices to the Wife's deceit. The old men had a dreadful time – but were also flattered by her assumed jealousy. God gave women skill to deceive effectively; somehow or other she always managed to dominate her husbands – even refusing her sexual favours.*

Lordinges, right thus, as ye have understonde,
Baar I stifly mine olde housbondes on honde                          380
That thus they seyden in hir dronkenesse;
And al was fals, but that I took witnesse
On Janekin, and on my nece also,
O Lord! The peyne I dide hem and the wo,
Ful giltelees, by Goddes sweete pine!                                385
For as an hors I koude bite and whine.
I koude pleyne, and yit was in the gilt,
Or elles often time hadde I been spilt,
Whoso that first to mille comth, first grint;
I pleyned first, so was oure werre ystint.                           390
They were ful glade to excuse hem blive
Of thing of which they nevere agilte hir live.
Of wenches wolde I beren hem on honde,
Whan that for sik unnethes mighte they stonde.
    Yet tikled I his herte, for that he                              395
Wende that I hadde of him so greet chiertee.
I swoor that al my walkinge out by nighte
Was for t'espie wenches that he dighte;
Under that colour hadde I many a mirthe.
For al swich wit is yeven us in oure birthe;                         400
Deceite, weping, spinning God hath yive
To wommen kindely, whil that they may live.
And thus of o thing I avaunte me,
Atte ende I hadde the bettre in ech degree,
By sleighte, or force, or by som maner thing,                       405
As by continueel murmur or grucching.
Namely abedde hadden they meschaunce:
Ther wolde I chide, and do hem no plesaunce;
I wolde no lenger in the bed abide,
If that I felte his arm over my side,                                410
Til he had maad his raunson unto me;
Thanne wolde I suffre him do his nicetee.

39

- Look closely at the analysis of married life that the Wife gives in lines 413-19. The Wife says she has 'won', but is this a victory that brings her happiness? Does she show some understanding of her own unpleasant behaviour? Does the language she uses offer insight into her attitude to sexual relationships?
- Try to imagine how infuriating her mockery must have been to her victim. Using the tone and setting that Chaucer presents here, write your own modern version of a conversation between a domineering wife and her husband.

| | |
|---|---|
| 415 | **With empty hand ... haukes lure** no falconer can persuade a hawk to return to him without some tempting bait |
| 417 | **make me a feyned appetit** pretend I enjoyed it |
| 418 | **bacon** tough old meat |
| 419 | **That made me ... wolde hem chide** this caused me to be bad-tempered with them all the time |
| 420-1 | **For thogh ... hir owene bord** if the pope himself sat next to them I would make them look fools at their own table |
| 422 | **I quitte hem** I paid them back |
| 424 | **make my testament** draw up my will [all debts and payments of debts might be listed there] |
| 426-8 | **I broghte it ... nevere been in reste** I used my wit so cleverly that they had to give up the argument, or else we would never have been finished |
| 429 | **wood leon** a mad lion |
| 430 | **faille of his conclusion** not get his own way |
| 431-2 | **Good lief ... oure sheep!** now, darling, just remember what a gentle expression Wilkin has on his face [Wilkin is presumably their ram, possibly castrated] |
| 433 | **ba thy cheke** kiss your cheek |
| 435 | **sweete, spiced conscience** anxiety to do what's right |
| 436-7 | **Sith ye so preche ... wel kan preche** you're always going on about the patience of Job, so you should be prepared to behave like him, since you preach about him so well |
| 440-2 | **Oon of us ... suffrable** it's obvious one of us has to give in, and, since a man is more reasonable than a woman, he must learn to put up with more |

*The Wife's method of triumphing over her husbands is spelt out – she must have her own way, or there will be perpetual war. She shows her power by laughing at her husband's distress; and she makes clear the lengths she is prepared to go in order to gain control in this way.*

And therfore every man this tale I telle,
Winne whoso may, for al is for to selle;
With empty hand men may none haukes lure.     415
For winning wolde I al his lust endure,
And make me a feyned appetit;
And yet in bacon hadde I nevere delit;
That made me that evere I wolde hem chide.
For thogh the pope hadde seten hem biside,     420
I wolde nat spare hem at hir owene bord;
For, by my trouthe, I quitte hem word for word.
As helpe me verray God omnipotent,
Though I right now sholde make my testament,
I ne owe hem nat a word that it nis quit.     425
I broghte it so aboute by my wit
That they moste yeve it up, as for the beste,
Or elles hadde we nevere been in reste.
For thogh he looked as a wood leon,
Yet sholde he faille of his conclusion.     430
   Thanne wolde I seye, "Goode lief, taak keep
How mekely looketh Wilkin, oure sheep!
Com neer, my spouse, lat me ba thy cheke!
Ye sholde been al pacient and meke,
And han a sweete spiced conscience,     435
Sith ye so preche of Jobes pacience.
Suffreth alwey, sin ye so wel kan preche;
And but ye do, certein we shal yow teche
That it is fair to have a wyf in pees.
Oon of us two moste bowen, doutelees;     440
And sith a man is moore resonable
Than womman is, ye moste been suffrable.

- Sex as a 'saleable commodity' has been referred to many times in the Wife's account of her manipulation of her older husbands. Consider how often she has spoken of using her sexual favours to get her own way. Note the language of buying and selling, and of the market place, that Chaucer has used in her life story. What is ironic about her comment (presumably to the last of her 'old men') that she could have gained great wealth and fine clothes by selling herself as a prostitute? Do you feel she has accurately assessed these early marriages as 'good'?
- Number four is presumably one of the 'bad' husbands. In lines 453-68 Chaucer both hints at her reason for objecting to him, and also suggests the methods she used to get her own back. Consider what these might have been, and how they add to our knowledge of the Wife's character. If he was so 'bad', how did she happen to marry him?

| | |
|---|---|
| **443-4** | **What eyleth yow ... my queynte allone?** what's wrong with you, complaining and groaning in this way? Is it because you want me to keep sexual favours exclusively for your pleasure? |
| **447-8** | **For if I ... as is a rose** if I chose to sell my body I could walk around in the finest clothes [*Belle chose* was a polite term for female sexual parts – contrast her coarse expression in line 444.] |

*'My fourthe housbonde was a revelour'*

| | |
|---|---|
| **451** | **hadde we on honde** we exchanged with one another |
| **453** | **revelour** someone who enjoys a lively [debauched?] social life |
| **454** | **paramour** mistress |
| **455** | **ragerie** strong passions |
| **456** | **Stibourn and strong, and joly as a pie** stubborn, strong-willed, and as lively as a magpie |
| **460** | **Metellius, the foule cherl, the swyn** Metellius, the wretched slave and swine [He appears in a tale by the Roman historian, Valerius Maximus, beating his wife to death for drinking too much. Presumably this tale was one the Wife was to hear from her fifth husband.] |
| **462** | **thogh I hadde been** if I had been |
| **463** | **daunted** stopped, frightened me off |
| **464-6** | **on Venus moste ... likerous tail** I begin to think of love [she means sex, really] for as surely as cold weather brings hail, so a mouth full of liquor prompts thoughts of lechery [The Wife seems to be excusing and offering explanations for her lack of restraint.] |
| **467** | **In wommen vinolent is no defence** women who have been drinking are unable to defend themselves [against the temptations of seduction] |

*The Wife asks why her old husband is so possessive: she will keep faithful to him in spite of the temptation. Her life with husband number four is introduced, as is her enjoyment of wine.*

What eyleth yow to grucche thus and grone?
Is it for ye wolde have my queynte allone?
Wy, taak it al! lo, have it every deel!                     445
Peter! I shrewe yow, but ye love it weel;
For if I wolde selle my *bele chose,*
I koude walke as fressh as is a rose;
But I wol kepe it for youre owene tooth.
Ye be to blame, by God! I sey yow sooth."                   450
    Swiche manere wordes hadde we on honde.
Now wol I speken of my fourthe housbonde.
    My fourthe housbonde was a revelour;
This is to seyn, he hadde a paramour;
And I was yong and ful of ragerie,                          455
Stibourn and strong, and joly as a pie.
How koude I daunce to an harpe smale,
And singe, ywis, as any nightingale,
Whan I had dronke a draughte of sweete wyn!
Metellius, the foule cherl, the swyn,                       460
That with a staf birafte his wyf hir lyf,
For she drank wyn, thogh I hadde been his wyf,
He sholde nat han daunted me fro drinke!
And after wyn on Venus moste I thinke,
For al so siker as cold engendreth hail,                    465
A likerous mouth moste han a likerous tail.
In wommen vinolent is no defence,—
This knowen lecchours by experience.

*'How koude I daunce to an harpe smale,*
*And singe, ywis, as any nightingale,*
*Whan I had dronke a draughte of sweete wyn'*

- In the first ten lines the Wife looks back on her youth. She says she has 'had my worlde' – in other words, made the most of it. How does Chaucer achieve a change of tone in these lines?
- Is she clear-sighted in her view of herself, her marriages and future prospects? List what she seems to have achieved, and what she seems to have missed out on. What would be your own recipe for a happy life? You could use the idea of an old man or woman looking back on earlier days as a basis for creative writing.
- Discuss whether she had any fondness for husband number four at all, using evidence from lines 480-502.

| 469 | **remembreth me** comes to my mind |
| 471 | **ticklethe me aboute myn herte roote** warms the cockles of my heart |
| 474 | **envenime** poisons and destroys |
| 475 | **Hath me biraft my beautee and my pith** has taken from me my beauty and my vigour |
| 477 | **flour** flour |
| 478 | **bren** bran [coarse husks left when the best of the grain has been taken] |
| 481 | **despit** anger |
| 483 | **he was quit** he was paid back for it |
| | **Seint Joce** [St Judocus, a Breton saint, possibly known to the Wife from her trips abroad.] |
| 484 | **I made him of the same wode a croce** I treated him to some of his own medicine [*literally:* I made him a cross of the same wood] |
| 485 | **Nat of my body** [The Wife is saying she was never physically unfaithful to her husband.] |
| 486-8 | **I made folk ... verray jalousie** I was so friendly and sociable towards other |

men that I made him stew in his own juice [*literally:* fry in his own grease] in absolute jealousy

| 489 | **purgatorie** miseries of purgatory [suffered for a time after death by those who have sinned in this world. She has made his life so wretched that he is likely to go straight to paradise.] |
| 492 | **his shoo ful bitterly him wrong** he was so tormented [*literally:* his shoe pinched him so painfully] |
| 494 | **wise** ways |
| | **I him twiste** I tortured him |
| 495 | **deyde** died |
| 496 | **lith ygrave under the roode beem** lies buried under the rood beam [at the edge of the chancel, and probably less expensive than a tomb in the chancel itself] |
| 498 | **Darius ... Appelles** [Appelles, a Greek craftsman, supposedly constructed a rich and wonderful tomb for King Darius.] |

*The Wife looks back fondly at her behaviour when she was young and beautiful; now she must use*
*those assets she has left as best she can. She paid her fourth husband back by making him furiously*
*jealous and extremely miserable. He died while she was on a pilgrimage to Jerusalem.*

But, Lord Crist! whan that it remembreth me
Upon my yowthe, and on my jolitee,                       470
It tikleth me aboute myn herte roote.
Unto this day it dooth myn herte boote
That I have had my world as in my time.
But age, allas, that al wole envenime,
Hath me biraft my beautee and my pith.                   475
Lat go, farewel; the devel go therwith!
The flour is goon, ther is namoore to telle;
The bren, as I best kan, now moste I selle;
But yet to be right mirie wol I fonde.
Now wol I tellen of my fourthe housbonde.                480
  I seye, I hadde in herte greet despit
That he of any oother had delit.
But he was quit, by God and by Seint Joce!
I made him of the same wode a croce;
Nat of my body, in no foul manere,                       485
But certeinly, I made folk swich cheere
That in his owene grece I made him frie
For angre, and for verray jalousie.
By God! in erthe I was his purgatorie,
For which I hope his soule be in glorie.                  490
For, God it woot, he sat ful ofte and song,
Whan that his shoo ful bitterly him wrong.
Ther was no wight, save God and he, that wiste,
In many wise, how soore I him twiste.
He deyde whan I cam fro Jerusalem,                       495
And lith ygrave under the roode beem,
Al is his tombe noght so curius
As was the sepulcre of him Darius,
Which that Appelles wroghte subtilly;
It nis but wast to burye him preciously.                 500
Lat him fare wel, God yeve his soul reste!
He is now in his grave and in his cheste.

- The Wife begins to talk about her next husband, and then digresses almost immediately. Why has Chaucer structured her story-telling in this way? Does it seem to you to add anything to her Prologue?
- Begin to build up a character sketch of husband five from the information given.
- Discuss with a partner what the Wife says in lines 515-24. Do you agree? Can you imagine situations in which she might be right about women's natures? Do you feel she is right to suggest that such behaviour is peculiar to women?

| | |
|---|---|
| 505 | **mooste shrewe** the most unkind |
| 506 | **al by rewe** one after another |
| 509 | **therwithal** what is more |
| 514 | **daungerous** hard to please, sparing |
| 516 | **queynte fantasie** a strange fancy [use of 'queynte' suggests it is sexual] |
| 517 | **waite what thing** whatever thing |
| 520 | **Presse on us faste** persuade us urgently |
| 521-3 | **With daunger ... litel prys** we women show what we have to sell most grudgingly. Things offered at a high price are valued correspondingly. Those too cheaply bought are considered to be worth very little. |
| 526 | **no richesse** not for his riches [he was a poor man] |
| 527 | **a clerk of Oxenford** an Oxford student [Jankin had been for 'som |

time' a student at Oxford. He had left his studies, possibly through lack of funds, and was employed by one of the Wife's husbands as a clerical assistant. Even the most shrewd and successful business men and merchants were often unable to read or write. The Wife earlier called him an 'apprentice' but the word is used loosely.]

| | |
|---|---|
| 529 | **my gossib** my best friend [her name is Alys or Alisoun, as is the Wife's] |
| 531 | **my privetee** my most intimate secrets |
| 532 | **Bet than oure parisshe preest** better than our parish priest did [suggesting that the Wife did not tell her misdeeds to the priest in confession, as she should have done, though she enjoyed discussing them with her best friend] |

*The Wife speaks fondly of husband number five, even though he sometimes beat her. She says all women love best those things which are difficult to obtain – and this husband's love was such a thing. She begins to tell how she met him, through her good friend Alison.*

Now of my fifthe housbonde wol I telle.
God lete his soule nevere come in helle!
And yet was he to me the mooste shrewe;                    505
That feele I on my ribbes al by rewe,
And evere shal unto myn ending day.
But in oure bed he was so fressh and gay,
And therwithal so wel koude he me glose,
Whan that he wolde han my *bele chose*,                    510
That thogh he hadde me bete on every bon,
He koude winne again my love anon.
I trowe I loved him best, for that he
Was of his love daungerous to me.
We wommen han, if that I shal nat lie,                     515
In this matere a queynte fantasie;
Waite what thing we may nat lightly have,
Therafter wol we crie al day and crave.
Forbede us thing, and that desiren we;
Preesse on us faste, and thanne wol we fle.                520
With daunger oute we al oure chaffare;
Greet prees at market maketh deere ware,
And to greet cheep is holde at litel prys:
This knoweth every womman that is wys.
My fifthe housbonde, God his soule blesse!                 525
Which that I took for love, and no richesse,
He som time was a clerk of Oxenford,
And hadde left scole, and wente at hom to bord
With my gossib, dwellinge in oure toun;
God have hir soule! Hir name was Alisoun.                  530
She knew myn herte, and eek my privetee,
Bet than oure parisshe preest, so moot I thee!

- How does Chaucer make it quite clear, in lines 533-42, that the Wife enjoys her husband's embarrassment? What does such pleasure suggest about the relationship between them?
- Make a note of the activities she mentions in the next lines. There is a suggestion here, as there was when she defended her many marriages at the beginning of the Prologue, that she is defying criticism. Discuss the accusations that could be made against her by other people. Do you feel she can be excused at all?

533 **biwreyed I my conseil al** I told her all my secrets

535 **that sholde han cost his lyf** that could have cost him his life

540 **reed and hoot** red and hot

542 **so greet a privetee** such a private thing

543 **bifel** it happened

**ones in a Lente** once in Lent [a time for spiritual considerations rather than gadding about]

545 **gay** lively, sociable

551 **bettre leyser for to pleye** more time to enjoy myself

553-4 **What wiste ... what place?** how was I to know when and where my heart's delight would appear?

555-9 **Therfore ... scarlet gites** and so I attend vigils [evening services before saints' days], religious processions and plays, weddings and sermons, wearing my best scarlet dress

560-1 **Thise wormes ... never a deel** I can promise you worms and moths and bugs never had a chance of spoiling my clothes

562 **wostow why?** do you know why?

*The Wife pauses to reminisce about her behaviour during her earlier marriages – how she told her friend details that made her husbands furiously embarrassed, how she enjoyed herself socialising and travelling, and, most particularly, one special day during Lent when she and her friend and Jankin went for a walk in the fields.*

To hire biwreyed I my conseil al.
For hadde myn housbonde pissed on a wal,
Or doon a thyng that sholde han cost his lyf,                535
To hire, and to another worthy wyf,
And to my nece, which that I loved weel,
I wolde han toold his conseil every deel.
And so I dide ful often, God it woot,
That made his face often reed and hoot                       540
For verray shame, and blamed himself for he
Had toold to me so greet a privetee.
    And so bifel that ones in a Lente—
So often times I to my gossib wente,
For evere yet I loved to be gay,                             545
And for to walke in March, Averill, and May,
Fro hous to hous, to heere sondry talis—
That Jankin clerk, and my gossib dame Alis,
And I myself, into the feeldes wente.
Myn housbonde was at Londoun al that Lente;                  550
I hadde the bettre leyser for to pleye,
And for to se, and eek for to be seye
Of lusty folk. What wiste I wher my grace
Was shapen for to be, or in what place?
Therfore I made my visitaciouns                             555
To vigilies and to processiouns,
To preching eek, and to thise pilgrimages,
To pleyes of miracles, and to mariages,
And wered upon my gaye scarlet gites.
Thise wormes, ne thise motthes, ne thise mites,             560
Upon my peril, frete hem never a deel;
And wostow why? for they were used weel.

- What the Wife says in lines 563-80 seems a mixture of romance, fantasy, and hard-headed common-sense. The walk through the fields seems at odds with the suggestion that a spare man 'up one's sleeve' is a useful insurance policy. And the bizarre 'dream' once again links 'love' to sex and money. Discuss with a partner the way in which the dream might be interpreted.
- She clearly values old wives' tales on 'how to get your man'. Are these any different from the sort of advice to be found in magazines today? Do people still believe dreams have particular significance?
- The Wife felt little regret at the passing of husband number four – she has already told us she had no intention of splashing out on his burial. The description of his burial in lines 587-99 is perhaps worth presenting as a dramatic improvisation.

| | | | |
|---|---|---|---|
| 563 | **what happed me** what happened to me | 577 | **mette** dreamt |
| 565 | **swich daliance** such flirtation | 578 | **wolde han slain me** would have killed me [She's clearly thinking of a sexual conquest.] |
| 566 | **purveiance** foresight, future plans | | |
| 569 | **bobance** boasting | 578 | **lay upright** lay on her back |
| 572-4 | **I holde ... is al ydo** I consider it totally stupid [*literally:* not worth a leek] to be like a mouse with just one hole to run down; if that one is stopped up all is lost | 581 | **bitokeneth** stands for, represents |
| | | 582 | **al was fals** it was all lies |
| | | 583-4 | **But as ... othere thinges moore** I always took wise women's advice in this and many other matters |
| 575 | **bar hym on honde** tricked or persuaded him into believing | 588 | **algate** none the less |
| 576 | **my dame** possibly mother, friend [dame Alys], or simply female trickery | 589 | **mooten** must |
| | | | **usage** the custom |
| | **soutiltee** subtlety, cunning | 591 | **But for that I was purveyed of a make** since I was already fixed up with a new husband |

50

*One fateful day the Wife makes her wishes clear to Jankin, and, in accordance with the feminine wiles she has acquired, makes up a story with which to entrap him. Caught up in memories of their courtship, she picks up the threads of her story on the day of husband number four's funeral.*

Now wol I tellen forth what happed me.
I seye that in the feeldes walked we,
Til trewely we hadde swich daliance,                        565
This clerk and I, that of my purveiance
I spak to him and seyde him how that he,
If I were widwe, sholde wedde me.
For certeinly, I sey for no bobance,
Yet was I nevere withouten purveiance                       570
Of mariage, n'of othere thinges eek.
I holde a mouses herte nat worth a leek
That hath but oon hole for to sterte to,
And if that faille, thanne is al ydo.
    I bar hym on honde he hadde enchanted me,—             575
My dame taughte me that soutiltee.
And eek I seyde I mette of him al night,
He wolde han slain me as I lay upright,
And al my bed was ful of verray blood;
But yet I hope that he shal do me good,                      580
For blood bitokeneth gold, as me was taught.
And al was fals; I dremed of it right naught,
But as I folwed ay my dames loore,
As wel of this as of othere thinges moore.
But now, sire, lat me se, what I shal seyn?                  585
A ha! by God, I have my tale ageyn.
    Whan that my fourthe housbande was on beere,
I weep algate, and made sory cheere,
As wives mooten, for it is usage,
And with my coverchief covered my visage,                   590
But for that I was purveyed of a make,
I wepte but smal, and that I undertake.

- The word 'appetit' in line 623 gives an indication of the coarseness of the Wife's approach to life. Is she in danger of becoming too unpleasant to be funny? Is it at all possible to feel sorry for her?
- The sign of the zodiac under which a person was born, and the planets within the influence of that sign at the time of birth, were considered to have a profound effect on the personality of each individual. Do people still believe in such influences? Are horoscopes of any value? Write one for the Wife, as it might appear in a modern magazine. You could write either an 'in-depth' character analysis, or a piece for a particular week or day.

(Born under the sign of Taurus the bull, which belongs to the 'house' or influence of the planet Venus, love will figure largely in her make-up. Mars, also ascendant at her birth, explains her warlike and pugnacious nature.)

| 594 | **maden sorwe** mourned for him |
| 595 | **oon of tho** one of them |
| 597 | **beere** bier [for carrying coffin] |
| 598 | **so clene and faire** so fine and shapely |
| 599 | **I yaf unto his hoold** gave him her heart |
| 602 | **coltes tooth** a fondness for young men |
| 603 | **Gat-tothed I was** I had a gap between my front teeth [which, she suggests, men found attractive; supposedly a sign of flirtatiousness] |
| 604 | **the prente of seinte Venus seel** 'saint' Venus had marked me as one of her own |
| 606 | **wel bigon** well provided for [by her previous rich old husbands] |
| 608 | *quoniam* [euphemism – her husbands valued her sexual parts and prowess] |
| 609 | **al Venerien / In feelinge** my emotions are wholly influenced by Venus |

*'And Mars yaf me my sturdy hardinesse'*

| 610 | **myn herte is Marcien** my strength of will comes from the influence of Mars |
| 611 | **likerousnesse** lecherousness |
| 612 | **sturdy hardinesse** toughness, endurance |
| 613 | **Myn ascendent ... therinne** I was born under Taurus, planet Mars then rising |
| 615-6 | **I folwed ... constellacioun** I'm always headstrong because of this constellation [she claims this excuses her behaviour] |
| 617-20 | **That made ... privee place.** [The stars are thus responsible for her inability to deny any 'good fellow' access to her sexual charms.] |
| | **chambre of Venus** [euphemism for sexual parts] |
| 619 | **Martes mark** [bold, high colouring suggests Mars' influence] |
| 620 | **privee place** [possibly a hidden birth mark] |

*'Venus me yaf my lust, my likerousnesse'*

*She accounts for her personality and behaviour by the fact that she was born under the influence of Venus and Mars.*

---

    To chirche was myn housbonde born a-morwe
With neighebores, that for him maden sorwe;
And Jankin, oure clerk, was oon of tho.          595
As help me God! whan that I saugh him go
After the beere, me thoughte he hadde a paire
Of legges and of feet so clene and faire
That al myn herte I yaf unto his hoold.
He was, I trowe, a twenty winter oold,        600
And I was fourty, if I shal seye sooth;
But yet I hadde alwey a coltes tooth.
Gat-tothed I was, and that bicam me weel;
I hadde the prente of seinte Venus seel.
As help me God! I was a lusty oon,         605
And faire, and riche, and yong, and wel bigon;
And trewely, as mine housbondes tolde me,
I hadde the beste *quoniam* mighte be.
For certes, I am al Venerien
In feelinge, and myn herte is Marcien.        610
Venus me yaf my lust, my likerousnesse,
And Mars yaf me my sturdy hardinesse;
Myn ascendent was Taur, and Mars therinne.
Allas, allas, that evere love was sinne!
I folwed ay myn inclinacioun         615
By vertu of my constellacioun;
That made me I koude noght withdrawe
My chambre of Venus from a good felawe.
Yet have I Martes mark upon my face,
And also in another privee place.        620
For God so wys be my savacioun,
I ne loved nevere by no discrecioun,
But evere folwede myn appetit,
Al were he short, or long, or blak, or whit;
I took no kep, so that he liked me,        625
How poore he was, ne eek of what degree.

In 1384 King Richard II, a cultured and often extravagant monarch, was the proud possessor of 12 books of romances. Books were still hand-written, and the finest were beautifully illuminated. A penniless clerk like Jankin would, therefore, treasure his book greatly. He may even have copied out his collection himself. Anthologies and collections of tales and extracts were popular in the fourteenth century. This collection clearly criticised disobedient and headstrong women. The Wife has to defend herself against the forces of ancient scholarship as well as against her critical young husband.

• Write your own modern alternative to the anti-feminist rhyme in lines 655-8, using a a similar rhyme scheme.

628 **hende** attractive, attentive, charming, pleasing [a term of approval and admiration, possibly also meaning available or handy – no wonder she married him!]

629 **solempnitee** elaborate ceremony

630 **lond and fee** land and possessions

633 **He nolde suffre nothing of my list** he would not let me have anything I wanted

634 **on the list** on the ear [*literally:* listener]

635 **For that ... a leef** because I tore a leaf from his book

637 **stibourn** stubborn

638 **of my tonge ... jangleresse** drove him mad with talk and nagging

640 **he had it sworn** he had sworn he would not let me do this

642 **Romain geestes** stories from Roman history .

643 **he, Simplicius Gallus** the man, Simplicius Gallus [another story from Valerius Maximus – see line 460]

645 **open-heveded he hir say** he saw her bare-headed

646 **upon a day** one day

648 **at a someres game** at the summer games or midsummer festival

649 **his witing** his knowledge

652 **forbedeth faste** strongly forbids

653 **go roule aboute** gad about

[Ecclesiastes 25 verse 25 tells men to stop wicked women travelling]

655-8 '**Whoso ... galwes!**' any fool stupid enough to build his house of willow branches, or spur a blind horse into a gallop over broken ground, or allow his wife to go travelling abroad, deserves to be hanged from the gallows!

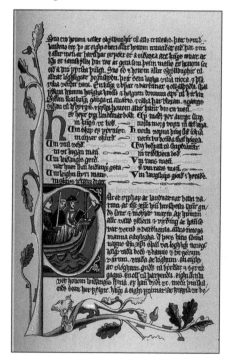

*'He hadde a book that gladly, night and day, For his desport he wolde rede alway'*

54

*Her speedy marriage to Jankin rapidly becomes acrimonious, as he abuses her, physically and verbally, once he has obtained control of all her goods. For her part she fully intends to continue to behave as she has always done before.*

What sholde I seye? But, at the monthes ende,
This joly clerk, Jankin, that was so hende,
Hath wedded me with greet solempnitee;
And to him yaf I al the lond and fee                           630
That evere was me yeven therbifoore.
But afterward repented me ful soore;
He nolde suffre nothing of my list.
By God! he smoot me ones on the list,
For that I rente out of his book a leef,                        635
That of the strook myn ere wax al deef.
Stibourn I was as is a leonesse,
And of my tonge a verray jangleresse,
And walke I wolde, as I had doon biforn,
From hous to hous, although he had it sworn;                    640
For which he often times wolde preche,
And me of olde Romain geestes teche;
How he Simplicius Gallus lefte his wyf,
And hire forsook for terme of al his lyf,
Noght but for open-heveded he hir say                          645
Lookinge out at his dore upon a day.
    Another Romain tolde he me by name,
That, for his wyf was at a someres game
Withouten his witing, he forsook hire eke.
And thanne wolde he upon his Bible seke                         650
That ilke proverbe of Ecclesiaste
Where he comandeth, and forbedeth faste,
Man shal nat suffre his wyf go roule aboute.
Thanne wolde he seye right thus, withouten doute:
    "Whoso that buildeth his hous al of salwes,                 655
And priketh his blinde hors over the falwes,
And suffreth his wyf to go seken halwes,
Is worthy to been hanged on the galwes!"

Jankin's 'book of wicked wives' clearly gives him hours of fun and entertainment, although it was not necessarily written for this purpose. As a 'clerk' Jankin would almost certainly have received his education from the church. Many scholars were already members of monastic orders, but Jankin could possibly have been one of the clever, but not wealthy, boys who were educated at the 300-400 grammar schools in England, which had been set up under the auspices of monks and cathedrals. Such boys generally proceeded to the universities of Oxford or Cambridge, where their studies continued, and where they enjoyed the protection of the church. Not all of these educated young men, however, really wanted to become priests, who were expected to live a life of chastity and purity. Many moved into employment as administrators or accountants, sometimes working, as Jankin does, for rich businessmen who were themselves unable to read or write.

Church writings and other influences on young clerks would have suggested that a celibate and priestly life was preferable to one involving women. Many anthologies of tales were produced suggesting that women were nothing but trouble.

671 **Valerie and Theofraste** were two separate works against marriage: the first, the epistle of Valerius on not taking a wife, by Walter Map; the second possibly by Theophrastus, friend of Aristotle, on the state of marriage. Much of what Chaucer incorporates into the Wife's complaint comes directly from this source.

674-7 Some of the other writers mentioned here write in favour of love, passion and marriage. Although **St Jerome** strongly opposed pleasures of the flesh, **Jovinian**, whose ideas the saint dismissed as absurd, was a rebel monk of the fifth century, who favoured marriage over virginity, and the enjoyment of food over fasting. **Tertullian** was a Roman Christian who supported chastity and monogamy, but **Crisippus** apparently favoured marriage – he too was dismissed as ridiculous by St Jerome. By contrast, **Trotula** has been identified as a learned Italian midwife of the eleventh century, who wrote about women's illnesses and passions. **Heloise** became the prioress of the convent at Argenteuil, in France. Her marriage to the great medieval scholar Peter Abelard was dissolved, partly because she herself objected to mixing marriage with philosophy – she nevertheless preserved her love for him until death. The story of Abelard's castration would have been well known, and would have offered another reminder of the potential dangers of matrimony.

679-80 The Wife also mentions the Book of Proverbs (**Parables of Salomon**) and Ovid's celebration of earthly love, the *Ars Amatoria* (**Ovides Art**).

659-60 **I sette ... olde sawe** I cared nothing at all for his proverbs or his wise old sayings

664-5 **This made ... in no cas** this made him absolutely furious with me; I completely refused to be corrected by him in any way whatsoever

666 **Seint Thomas** St Thomas à Becket

670 **his desport** his entertainment

671 **he cleped it** he called it

672 **lough alwey ful faste** always laughed very heartily

674 **that highte** who was called

681 **o volume** one volume

688 **trusteth wel** believe me

690 **But if it be ... lives** Unless it is the lives of holy [female] saints

*The Wife resents her young husband's criticisms of her behaviour, and suggests most women would feel the same. She explores more fully the details of the marital dispute centring around Jankin's hated book.*

But al for noght, I sette noght an hawe
Of his proverbes n'of his olde sawe,                        660
Ne I wolde nat of him corrected be.
I hate him that my vices telleth me,
And so doo mo, God woot, of us than I.
This made him with me wood al outrely;
I nolde noght forbere him in no cas.                        665
    Now wol I sey yow sooth, by Seint Thomas,
Why that I rente out of his book a leef,
For which he smoot me so that I was deef.
    He hadde a book that gladly, night and day,
For his desport he wolde rede alway;                        670
He cleped it Valerie and Theofraste,
At which book he lough alwey ful faste.
And eek ther was somtime a clerk at Rome,
A cardinal, that highte Seint Jerome,
That made a book again Jovinian;                            675
In which book eek ther was Tertulan,
Crisippus, Trotula, and Helowis,
That was abbesse nat fer fro Paris;
And eek the Parables of Salomon,
Ovides Art, and bookes many on,                             680
And alle thise were bounden in o volume.
And every night and day was his custume,
Whan he hadde leyser and vacacioun
From oother worldly occupacioun,
To reden on this book of wikked wives.                      685
He knew of hem mo legendes and lives
Than been of goode wives in the Bible.
For trusteth wel, it is an impossible
That any clerk wol speke good of wives,
But if it be of hooly seintes lives,                        690
Ne of noon oother womman never the mo.

- The Wife is furious that women should be so criticised, simply because all books were written by men. If women could write books, she says, they could find plenty of tales to illustrate the wickedness of men. In your experience do female writers make the wickedness of men their subject matter? The first tale in Jankin's book is that of Eve, who 'brought all mankind to wretchedness' by her actions. Is it possible to rewrite the story of Adam and Eve, giving Eve a more sympathetic hearing, without altering the basic facts of the tale?
- If, as Chaucer implies in line 692, the way a work of art, or a piece of literature, is created has more to do with the prejudices of the creator than with reality, what would the Wife's Tale and Prologue have been like if the Canterbury Tales had been written by a woman?
- Undoubtedly men had control of the world of scholarship (even though the Wife herself has mentioned two extremely influential and intelligent women – see line 677). Does the evidence of this Prologue so far suggest that women were downtrodden and inferior? Is intellectual superiority the most effective way of gaining power?

| | |
|---|---|
| 692 | **Who peyntede the leon, tel me who?** [Aesop's fable tells of a man-made sculpture of a lion conquered by a man; if a lion had been the sculptor he would have shown that the contest might well have had a different outcome.] |
| 694 | **withinne hire oratories** closeted in their monastic cells |
| 696 | **the mark ... may redresse** men [those who carry the mark of Adam] can put right |
| 697-8 | **The children ... ful contrarius** those born under the influence of the two opposing planets [scholars under the sign of Mercury, passionate women under the sign of Venus] have completely different outlooks on life |
| 700 | **dispence** extravagant expenditure |
| 701 | **for** because of |
| 702-4 | **Ech falleth ... exaltat** when one of these planets is at its highest point in the sky [and therefore at its most |

influential] the other is at its lowest - for example, when the sun is in the sign of Pisces, Venus is at its height, whilst Mercury is fallen

707-10 **The clerk ... kepe hir mariage** when the clerk or scholar is too old to be able to enjoy sexual pleasure he will sit down and spend his old age writing about how women cannot remain faithful to their marriage vows

713 **Jankin, that was oure sire** Jankin, the lord and master of the house

718 **boghte us ... again** [Adam and Eve were cast out of Paradise because of disobeying God, when Eve picked the forbidden fruit and gave it to Adam. Christ's death on the cross was the sacrifice which redeemed humanity, and gave mankind the chance of divine forgiveness.]

719-20 **expres of womman** it is particularly stated that the woman caused this downfall

*The Wife claims antagonism between women and scholars is inevitable, since they are ruled by opposing planets. She also suggests that old scholars, no longer able to enjoy sexual pleasures, write sour attacks against women out of the bitterness of their own impotence. She then describes the night of her fight with Jankin in even more detail.*

Who peyntede the leon, tel me who?
By God! if wommen hadde writen stories,
As clerkes han withinne hire oratories,
They wolde han writen of men moore wikkednesse          695
Than al the mark of Adam may redresse.
The children of Mercurie and of Venus
Been in hir wirking ful contrarius;
Mercurie loveth wisdam and science,
And Venus loveth riot and dispence.                     700
And, for hire diverse disposicioun,
Ech falleth in otheres exaltacioun.
And thus, God woot, Mercurie is desolat
In Pisces, wher Venus is exaltat;
And Venus falleth ther Mercurie is reysed.              705
Therfore no womman of no clerk is preysed.
The clerk, whan he is oold, and may noght do
Of Venus werkes worth his olde sho,
Thanne sit he doun, and writ in his dotage
That wommen kan nat kepe hir mariage.                   710
   But now to purpos, why I tolde thee
That I was beten for a book, pardee!
Upon a night Jankin, that was oure sire,
Redde on his book, as he sat by the fire,
Of Eva first, that for hir wikkednesse                  715
Was al mankinde broght to wrecchednesse,
For which that Jhesu Crist himself was slain,
That boghte us with his herte blood again.
Lo, heere expres of womman may ye finde,
That womman was the los of al mankinde.                 720

• The stories on this page and the following one have been collected from various places: what aspects of women do they criticise?

721-3    The Old Testament story tells how Delila betrayed **Samson** to the Philistines by cutting off his long hair (source of his mighty strength) while he slept.

724-6    The shirt that **Deianira**, Hercules' wife, gave him had been dipped in deadly poison by the centaur Nessus. She thought it held magic to make Hercules love her again. Instead it clung to his skin, causing him such pain and torment that he chose to be burnt alive.

728-32   According to the writings of St Jerome, the philosopher **Socrates** had a second wife, **Xanthippe**, a terrible scold, who once threw the contents of a chamber pot at him.

733-6    The legend of **Pasiphae**, wife of Minos of Crete, tells how she developed an unnatural passion for a white bull, given to Minos by Poseidon, the sea-god. She bore the bull a son, the Minotaur.

737-9    Returning after ten years from the Trojan wars, Agamemnon found his wife, **Clytemnestra**, had taken a new lover, Aegisthos. Wife and lover murdered the husband in his bath.

740-6    **Amphiaraos** was one of the ill-fated seven warriors, who set out to take Thebes for Polynaikos. Originally reluctant to take part in the attack, Amphiaraos was persuaded by his wife, **Eriphyle**. She had taken bribes

from Polynaikos to gain this support, in spite of knowing that, if her husband went, his death had been ordained. He was struck by lightning outside the city gate.

722     **his lemman kitte it** his lover cut it

723     **bothe his yen** both his eyes

724     **tho redde he me** then he read to me

727     **no thing forgat he** he left out no part of

730     **sely man** innocent man [but perhaps silly too]

731     **namoore dorste he seyn** he dared say no more than this

732     **'Er that thonder stinte, comth a reyn'** rain comes before the thunder [her shouting] stops

734     **For shrewednesse ... swete** he relished this tale as a fine example of female wickedness

735-6   **Fy! spek namoore ... liking** for goodness' sake no more! The story of her unnatural lust and affection is a horrible thing

739     **ful good devocioun** with great attention

740     **for what occasioun** how it happened that

743     **ouche of golde** gold-clasped necklace

744     **prively** secretly

746     **sory grace** a wretched fate.

*More stories of deceitful or unpleasant wives are read to the angry wife by her husband.*

Tho redde he me how Sampson loste his heres:
Slepinge, his lemman kitte it with hir sheres;
Thurgh which treson loste he bothe his yen.
    Tho redde he me, if that I shal nat lyen,
Of Hercules and of his Dianire,                             725
That caused hym to sette hymself afire.
    No thing forgat he the care and the wo
That Socrates hadde with his wives two;
How Xantippa caste pisse upon his heed.
This sely man sat stille as he were deed;                   730
He wiped his heed, namoore dorste he seyn,
But "Er that thonder stinte, comth a reyn!"
    Of Phasipha, that was the queene of Crete,
For shrewednesse, him thoughte the tale swete;
Fy! spek namoore—it is a grisly thyng—                      735
Of hire horrible lust and hir liking.
    Of Clitermystra, for hire lecherie,
That falsly made hire housbonde for to die,
He redde it with ful good devocioun.
    He tolde me eek for what occasioun                       740
Amphiorax at Thebes loste his lyf.
Myn housbonde hadde a legende of his wyf,
Eriphilem, that for an ouche of gold
Hath prively unto the Grekes told
Wher that hir housbonde hidde him in a place,               745
For which he hadde at Thebes sory grace.

- Chaucer has cast his net widely in these examples of wicked women: some come from the Bible, some from classical mythology and others from the writings of church elders, or history books. Do you think this book of Jankin's actually existed? And if not, why did Chaucer invent it? What reasons might he have for assuming that not only the Wife herself, but also her audience would know these stories?

747-51 **Livilla** was persuaded to poison her husband, Drusus, by her lover, Sejanus - minister to the Roman Emperor Tiberius Claudius Nero in AD 23.

747-55 Lucretius, the Roman poet, was given a love-potion by his wife, **Lucilia**, which had the effect of sending him mad and causing him to die.

757-64 The story of the man **Latumius** and the hanging tree derived from the works of Cicero, and appeared in a popular medieval collection of stories used in sermons.

749 **That oon, ... for hate** one for love, the other for hate

750 **on an even late** late one evening

751 **his fo** his enemy

752 **likerous** lecherous

753 **for he sholde** so that he would

755 **That he was ... the morwe** he had died from it before the next day

756 **algates** in every way

761 **for herte despitus** because their hearts were wretched

762 **leeve brother** dear brother

763 **yif me a plante** give me a cutting

766-8 **That somme ... floor upright** that some had killed their husbands in their own bed and then spent the whole night with a lover, while the corpse lay face upwards on the floor

769 **drive nailes in hir brain** [The Bible story of Sisera (Judges 4 verse 21) tells how she killed Jael by hammering a nail into his head.]

775-7 **'Bet is ... for to chide'** it's better to make your home with a lion or a terrible dragon than with a nagging woman

778-81 **'Bet is ... loven ay'** it's better to hide away up in the attic than live in the house, if there's a bad-tempered wife there; women are so wicked and contrary that they make a point of always hating what their husbands enjoy.

*More stories of wretched wives are listed, followed by male jokes about unhappy marriages.*

Of Livia tolde he me, and of Lucie:
They bothe made hir housbondes for to die;
That oon for love, that oother was for hate.
Livia hir housbonde, on an even late,                    750
Empoisoned hath, for that she was his fo;
Lucia, likerous, loved hire housbonde so
That, for he sholde alwey upon hire thinke,
She yaf him swich a manere love-drinke
That he was deed er it were by the morwe;               755
And thus algates housbondes han sorwe.
    Thanne tolde he me how oon Latumius
Compleyned unto his felawe Arrius
That in his gardin growed swich a tree
On which he seyde how that his wives thre              760
Hanged hemself for herte despitus.
"O leeve brother," quod this Arrius,
"Yif me a plante of thilke blissed tree,
And in my gardin planted shal it bee."
    Of latter date, of wives hath he red               765
That somme han slain hir housbondes in hir bed,
And lete hir lecchour dighte hire al the night,
Whan that the corps lay in the floor upright.
And somme han drive nailes in hir brain,
Whil that they slepte, and thus they had hem slain.    770
Somme han hem yeve poisoun in hire drinke.
He spak moore harm than herte may bithinke;
And therwithal he knew of mo proverbes
Than in this world ther growen gras or herbes.
"Bet is," quod he, "thyn habitacioun                   775
Be with a leon or a foul dragoun,
Than with a womman usinge for to chide."
"Bet is," quod he, "hye in the roof abide,
Than with an angry wyf doun in the hous;
They been so wikked and contrarious,                   780
They haten that hir housbondes loven ay."

- Chaucer has been preparing his audience for the scene of marital strife from the moment he mentioned the Wife's deafness in the General Prologue. Do you find it amusing? or disturbing? Consider how the scene might be presented on stage.
- Do you consider the Wife was justified in taking offence at what her husband read out? How far is this episode more than just a battle between one man and his wife?

782-3   **'a womman ... of hir smok'** a woman loses all modesty when she takes off all her clothes

784-5   **'A fair womman ... in a sowes nose'** finding a beautiful woman who is also chaste is as rare as finding a gold ring in a pig's nose

786   **wolde wene** could imagine

787   **pine** the agony

788   **saugh he wolde nevere fine** saw he would never stop [finish]

790   **plight** snatched

791   **right as he radde** whilst he was reading

792   **fest** fist

      **cheke** cheek

793   **he fil** he fell

794-5   **And he up ... on the heed** up he jumped like a wild lion, and hit me on the head with his fist

796   **That in ... I were deed** so that I fell on the floor as if dead

798   **agast** horrified

      **wolde han fled his wey** would have run away

799   **atte last. ... I breyde** finally I woke out of my swoon

800   **hastow** hast thou [have you]

801   **mordred** murdered

803   **kneled faire adoun** knelt down courteously [behaving in a way that pleases her at last]

804   **suster** sister [here meaning partner]

806   **it is thyself to wite** it's your own fault, you provoked me

807   **I thee biseke** I beseech you

808   **eftsoones** straight away

809   **thus muchel am I wreke** thus I get revenge

810   **I may no lenger speke** I can speak no more

*Exasperated by Jankin's proverbs and stories, the Wife snatches some pages from the book. Jankin hits her and is horrified when she pretends to be badly hurt.*

He seyde, "a womman cast hir shame away,
Whan she cast of hir smok"; and forthermo,
"A fair womman, but she be chaast also,
Is lyk a gold ring in a sowes nose."                    785
Who wolde wene, or who wolde suppose,
The wo that in myn herte was, and pine?
    And whan I saugh he wolde nevere fine
To reden on this cursed book al night,
Al sodeynly thre leves have I plight                    790
Out of his book, right as he radde, and eke
I with my fest so took him on the cheke
That in oure fyr he fil bakward adoun.
And he up stirte as dooth a wood leoun,
And with his fest he smoot me on the heed,              795
That in the floor I lay as I were deed.
And whan he saugh how stille that I lay,
He was agast, and wolde han fled his way,
Til atte laste out of my swogh I breyde.
"O, hastow slain me, false theef?" I seyde,             800
"And for my land thus hastow mordred me?
Er I be deed, yet wol I kisse thee."
    And neer he cam, and kneled faire adoun,
And seyde, "Deere suster Alisoun,
As help me God! I shal thee nevere smite.               805
That I have doon, it is thyself to wite.
Foryeve it me, and that I thee biseke!"
And yet eftsoones I hitte him on the cheke,
And seyde, "Theef, thus muchel am I wreke;
Now wol I die, I may no lenger speke."                  810

- The Wife recounts her version of the battle between herself and Jankin, and the subsequent peace treaty, with a certain complacency. Write your own version of events, as she might have told them to her friend Alison. Alternatively, you might wish to give Jankin's version of the story.
- The Friar calls the Wife's Prologue 'a long preamble of a tale' (line 831). In fact her Prologue is a tale itself – her own life story. Write an obituary for the Wife of Bath, using the factual details available, together with some conclusions about her personality.
- Look back to the boldness with which she opens her Prologue. She was prepared to tackle the accepted male power of the church and of learning. She seems triumphant at the end of her Prologue – what has she actually achieved?

| | | | |
|---|---|---|---|
| 811 | muchel a great deal of | 821 | Keep thyn ... myn estaat keep your reputation and maintain my status in society |
| 812 | fille acorded came to an agreement | | |
| 813 | yaf me al the bridel handed over complete control [*literally:* gave me the bridle completely] | 822 | debaat argument |
| | | 824 | Inde India |
| 814 | governance ordering, control | 826-7 | I prey to God ... mercy deere may the merciful God sitting in majesty bless Jankin's soul |
| 815 | of his tonge, and of his hond what he was allowed to say and do | | |
| 816 | brenne ... right tho burn his book right there and then | 829 | lough laughed |
| | | 830 | so have I joye or blis as I hope to gain heavenly joy or bliss |
| 818 | maistrie mastery | | |
| | soverainetee total domination | 831 | preamble of a tale introduction to a story |
| 820 | as thee lust as you wish | | |

*The Wife and Jankin come to an agreement about how the rest of their married life should proceed. The Wife's Prologue is almost done, and the Friar bursts out laughing at the length of it.*

But atte laste, with muchel care and wo,
We fille acorded by us selven two.
He yaf me al the bridel in myn hond,
To han the governance of hous and lond,
And of his tonge, and of his hond also;                          815
And made him brenne his book anon right tho.
And whan that I hadde geten unto me,
By maistrie, al the soverainetee,
And that he seyde, "Myn owene trewe wyf,
Do as thee lust the terme of al thy lyf;                         820
Keep thyn honour, and keep eek myn estaat"—
After that day we hadden never debaat.
God helpe me so, I was to him as kinde
As any wyf from Denmark unto Inde,
And also trewe, and so was he to me.                             825
I prey to God, that sit in magestee,
So blesse his soule for his mercy deere.
Now wol I seye my tale, if ye wol heere.'
   The Frere lough, whan he hadde herd al this;
'Now dame,' quod he, 'so have I joye or blis,                    830
This is a long preamble of a tale!'

- Clearly her audience has found the Wife's Prologue interesting and entertaining. She herself said her intention was 'to play'; but how serious is it all? How far is there a wider significance than for the Wife herself, in what she says and does?
- The Wife's story has been told in a very rambling manner. How has Chaucer made her digressions an important part of the character and way of life of this woman?
- Discuss how Chaucer uses these final lines to provide continuity, both with other parts of the complete *Canterbury Tales*, and as an effective bridge between the Wife's Prologue and the Tale that follows.

832    **gale** guffaw

833    **Goddes armes two** by God's arms [a coarse oath]

834    **A frere ... everemo** a friar will always push himself forward every time

837    **What spekestow of preambulacion?** what have you got to say about wandering about? [An oblique reference to the way friars travelled all over the country.]

838-9    **What! amble ... this manere** just walk off, or trot on, or keep quiet, or go and sit down! You're spoiling our entertainment by this behaviour

840    **woltow so** is that what you wish

844-7    **Now elles ... Sidingborne** now Friar, curse your face and curse myself, said the Summoner, if I fail to tell two or three stories about friars before we get to Sittingbourne [In fact the summoner does tell a tale of a greedy friar, but the rest of these promises are left unfulfilled.]

848    **I shal make ... to morne** you'll rue the day

849    **pacience** you won't hear it patiently

852    **Ye fare ... of ale** you're behaving like people who have drunk too much

855    **If I have ... worthy Frere** if this worthy Friar will give me permission

*Summoner and Friar bicker about the Friar's interruption to the Wife's tale, and agree to settle their differences later. The Host invites the Wife to continue.*

And whan the Somonour herde the Frere gale,
'Lo,' quod the Somonour, 'Goddes armes two!
A frere wol entremette him everemo.
Lo, goode men, a flie and eek a frere                                835
Wol falle in every dissh and eek mateere.
What spekestow of preambulacioun?
What! amble, or trotte, or pees, or go sit doun!
Thou lettest oure disport in this manere.'
  'Ye, woltow so, sire Somonour?' quod the Frere;        840
'Now, by my feith, I shal, er that I go,
Telle of a somonour swich a tale or two,
That alle the folk shal laughen in this place.'
  'Now elles, Frere, I bishrewe thy face,'
Quod this Somonour, 'and I bishrewe me,                         845
But if I telle tales two or thre
Of freres, er I come to Sidingborne,
That I shall make thyn herte for to morne,
For wel I woot thy pacience is gon.'
  Oure Hooste cride 'Pees! and that anon!'                 850
And seyde, 'Lat the womman telle hire tale.
Ye fare as folk that dronken ben of ale.
Do, dame, telle forth youre tale, and that is best.'
  'Al redy, sire,' quod she, 'right as yow lest,
If I have licence of this worthy Frere.'                               855
  'Yis, dame,' quod he, 'tel forth, and I wol heere.'

- What do the first five lines of the Tale suggest about the type of story the Wife might tell? And in what way does the rest of this page suggest something rather different?
- Unlike monks, friars travelled around the country preaching and hearing confessions. They lived by what they could earn or beg from those they visited. A 'limiter' was licensed to beg within a particular area. This system was open to abuse, and friars quickly gained a reputation for exploitation. Consider the ways in which the Wife's description of their activities is a satirical attack on the Friar.

859 **Al was this land fulfild of faierie** the whole land was filled full of fairies

862 **the olde opinion, as I rede** this is what people used to believe, as I understand

864 **now kan no man se none elves more** now no one can see any fairies at all [emphatic double negative]

868 **As thikke as motes in the sonne-beem** as thickly clustered as specks of dust in a sunbeam

869-71 **Blessinge ... daieries** friars seem to get everywhere, blessing halls, bedrooms, kitchens and private apartments, cities, towns, castles, towers, villages, barns, cowsheds and dairies

872 **This maketh ...** for this reason

873 **ther as wont to walken** where there used to walk

875 **undermeles and morweninges** afternoons and mornings

876 **seyth his ... thinges** recites holy offices

877 **limitacioun** area within which he may beg

878 **saufly** safely [fairy stories often tell of girls seduced by magical beings, who lure them away]

880-1 **Ther is noon ... but dishonour** he is the only incubus, and he will merely bring a girl dishonour [An incubus was a fairy lover – seduced by him a girl would have a child half-human, half-fairy. Seduction by the Friar brings only shame, nothing more.]

*The Tale is set in the time of King Arthur, when elves and fairies could still be found in the English countryside. The Wife suggests these have been chased away by the vast numbers of wandering friars who seem to be found everywhere.*

'In th'olde dayes of the King Arthour,
Of which that Britons speken greet honour,
Al was this land fulfild of faierie.
The elf-queene, with hir joly compaignie, 860
Daunced ful ofte in many a grene mede.
This was the olde opinion, as I rede;
I speke of manie hundred yeres ago.
But now kan no man se none elves mo,
For now the grete charitee and prayeres 865
Of limitours and othere hooly freres,
That serchen every lond and every streem,
As thikke as motes in the sonne-beem,
Blessinge halles, chambres, kitchenes, boures,
Citees, burghes, castels, hye toures, 870
Thropes, bernes, shipnes, daieries—
This maketh that ther ben no faieries.
For ther as wont to walken was an elf,
Ther walketh now the limitour himself,
In undermeles and in morweninges, 875
And seyth his matins and his hooly thinges
As he gooth in his limitacioun.
Wommen may go now saufly up and doun.
In every bussh or under every tree
Ther is noon oother incubus but he, 880
And he ne wol doon hem but dishonour.

- Fairy tales have traditional characteristics, some of which appear in the opening to this tale, but there are modes of behaviour here which seem out of place, although they fit well with the Wife's own attitude to life. How does the start of her story, on this page, seems to differ from the usual fairy tale?

| | | | |
|---|---|---|---|
| 882 | **so bifel it** it so happened | 893 | **Paraventure ... tho** perhaps that was the law in those times |
| 885 | **happed that** happened by chance that | 894 | **mo** more |
| 886 | **biforn** in front of him | 895 | **of grace** for mercy |
| 887 | **anon, ... hir heed** straight away, despite her pleas | 897 | **al at her wille** completely in her power |
| 888 | **he rafte hir maidenhed** he raped her [deprived her of her virginity] | 898 | **spille** spill [his blood] |
| 889 | **For which ... swich clamour** there was such outcry at this violation | 902 | **in swich array** in such a state |
| | | 903 | **suretee** guarantee |
| 890 | **pursute** petition | 906 | **Be war ... iren!** beware [be careful], keep your neck from the axe! |
| 891 | **dampned ... to be deed** this knight was condemned to death | 908 | **leve** permission |
| 892 | **by cours of lawe** according to law [Although the law against rape was most severe in thirteenth and fourteenth centuries – it was a crime punishable by blinding and castration – it was very seldom that such punishment was carried out.] | 909 | **seche and leer** search out and discover |
| | | 911-12 | **suretee ... in this place** before you go, I must have some guarantee that you will return and give yourself up |

*A knight rapes an innocent maiden. The law demands his death, but the queen asks Arthur to allow her to decide his punishment. She sets him a task: to discover what women most desire. Unless he finds the answer within the allotted time, he will die.*

And so bifel it that this king Arthour
Hadde in his hous a lusty bacheler,
That on a day cam ridinge fro river;
And happed that, allone as he was born,                   885
He saugh a maide walkinge him biforn,
Of which maide anon, maugree hir heed,
By verray force, he rafte hire maidenhed;
For which oppressioun was swich clamour
And swich pursute unto the king Arthour,                  890
That dampned was this knight for to be deed,
By cours of lawe, and sholde han lost his heed—
Paraventure swich was the statut tho—
But that the queene and othere ladies mo
So longe preyeden the king of grace,                      895
Til he his lyf him graunted in the place,
And yaf him to the queene, al at hir wille,
To chese wheither she wolde him save or spille.
    The queene thanketh the king with al hir might,
And after this thus spak she to the knight,               900
Whan that she saugh hir time, upon a day:
"Thou standest yet," quod she, "in swich array
That of thy lyf yet hastow no suretee.
I grante thee lyf, if thou kanst tellen me
What thing is it that wommen moost desiren.               905
Be war, and keep thy nekke-boon from iren!
And if thou kanst nat tellen it anon,
Yet wol I yeve thee leve for to gon
A twelf-month and a day, to seche and leere
An answere suffisant in this mateere;                     910
And suretee wol I han, er that thou pace,
Thy body for to yelden in this place."

• The list of what is pleasing to women has a familiar ring. How closely does it correspond to things already mentioned in the Wife's Prologue? Is it correct to state these things give women greatest pleasure? Would the list for men be different?

913    **Wo** wretched
      **siketh** sighed

914    **But what** even so, nevertheless
      **as him liketh** just as he pleases

915    **chees him for to wende** he chose to set out

917    **as God wolde him purveye** that God might provide him with [having taken his pleasure by force, the knight is now just a pawn in the hands of God and of his women judges]

919    **seketh** searched

920    **finde grace** find assistance, help and consolation

922    **in no coost** in no place [*literally:* on no side]

924    **accordinge in-feere** in agreement

926    **honour** dignity, respect
      **jolinesse** a merry life

927    **array** clothes
      **lust abedde** a lively sex life

928    **oftetime to be widwe and wedde** to be widowed and re-married several times

930    **yflatered and yplesed** flattered and complimented

931    **ny the sothe** near the truth

933-4   **with attendance ... moore and lesse** women of both high and low degree are caught by men who dance attendance and make a fuss of them

936    **right as us lest** just as we please

937    **repreve** criticise, condemn

938    **no thing nice** not at all foolish

939    **trewely** in all truth

940-1   **If any wight ... us sooth** if anyone should criticise a fault [*literally:* hit us on a tender spot] there is no woman living who would not lash out at him for speaking the truth

942    **assay** just try it

943-4   **be we never ... clene of sinne** however sinful we are secretly, we like to be thought wise and pure

*Reluctantly, the knight agrees to accept the task, and sets out to discover what women want most. They seem to want all sorts of different things.*

Wo was this knight, and sorwefully he siketh;
But what, he may nat do al as him liketh.
And at the laste he chees him for to wende,                        915
And come again, right at the yeres ende,
With swich answere as God wolde him purveye;
And taketh his leve, and wendeth forth his weye.
  He seketh every hous and every place
Where as he hopeth for to finde grace,                             920
To lerne what thing wommen loven moost;
But he ne koude arriven in no coost
Wher as he mighte finde in this mateere
Two creatures accordinge in-feere.
Somme seyde wommen loven best richesse,                            925
Somme seyde honour, somme seyde jolinesse,
Somme riche array, somme seyden lust abedde,
And oftetime to be widwe and wedde.
Somme seyde that oure hertes been moost esed
Whan that we been yflatered and yplesed.                           930
He gooth ful ny the sothe, I wol nat lie.
A man shal winne us best with flaterie;
And with attendance, and with bisinese,
Been we ylimed, bothe moore and lesse.
  And somme seyen that we loven best                       935
For to be free, and do right as us lest,
And that no man repreve us of oure vice,
But seye that we be wise, and no thing nice.
For trewely ther is noon of us alle,
If any wight wol clawe us on the galle,                            940
That we nel kike, for he seith us sooth.
Assay, and he shal finde it that so dooth;
For, be we never so vicious withinne,
We wol been holden wise and clene of sinne.

This story is most appropriate to the Wife of Bath. We know she is indiscreet, as is the wife of Midas. In her Prologue she manipulates information to improve her own argument, and here she alters the tale of Midas by making him reveal the secret of his ass's ears to his wife, not his barber. (Or rather, Chaucer alters the story, thus giving it a more anti-feminist slant.) Moreover, the Wife and Midas have things in common – a love of gold, an appetite for high living, and an inability to distinguish between coarse pleasures and those more spiritually satisfying. He was given his ass's ears because he preferred the pipes of Pan to the divine music of Apollo; like the Wife herself, his ears were not attuned to the finer things of life.

945 **han** have

946 **stable and eek secree** unchangeable and also discreet

947 **o purpos** to remain steadfast to one purpose

948 **biwreye** betray

949 **a rake-stele** an old rake's handle

950 **hele** keep to ourselves

951 **Mida** Midas [mythical king of Lydia]

952 **Ovide** Ovid [classical writer of a collection of myths, the *Metamorphoses*]

**thinges smale** little stories

957 **ther wiste of it namo** no one else knew of it

960 **disfigure** disfigurement

961-3 **She swoor ... foul a name** she swore she would not so destroy her husband's good name, not for the whole world

965 **nathelees** nevertheless

**that she dide** that she would die

966 **a conseil** a secret

967-8 **it swal so ... moste asterte** her heart swelled so, that surely the words must burst out

969 **sith** since

970 **mareys** marshland

972 **as a bitore bombleth in the mire** just like a bittern booming in the fenlands

974 **biwreye me nat** don't betray me

977 **al hool** completely sound

*Some say women like to be considered discreet. The Wife disagrees, telling her version of the tale of Midas and his ass's ears as proof.*

And somme seyn that greet delit han we 945
For to been holden stable, and eek secree,
And in o purpos stedefastly to dwelle,
And nat biwreye thing that men us telle.
But that tale is nat worth a rake-stele.
Pardee, we wommen konne no thing hele; 950
Witnesse on Mida,—wol ye heere the tale?
    Ovide, amonges othere thinges smale,
Seyde Mida hadde, under his longe heres,
Growinge upon his heed two asses eres,
The whiche vice he hidde, as he best mighte, 955
Ful subtilly from every mannes sighte,
That, save his wyf, ther wiste of it namo.
He loved hire moost, and trusted hire also;
He preyed hire that to no creature
She sholde tellen of his disfigure. 960
    She swoor him nay, for al this world to winne,
She nolde do that vileynie or sinne,
To make hir housbonde han so foul a name.
She nolde nat telle it for hir owene shame.
But natheless, hir thoughte that she dide, 965
That she so longe sholde a conseil hide;
Hir thoughte it swal so soore aboute hir herte
That nedely som word hire moste asterte;
And sith she dorste telle it to no man,
Doun to a mareys faste by she ran— 970
Til she cam there, hir herte was a-fire—
And as a bitore bombleth in the mire,
She leyde hir mouth unto the water doun:
"Biwreye me nat, thou water, with thy soun,"
Quod she; "to thee I telle it and namo; 975
Myn housbonde hath longe asses eris two!
Now is myn herte al hool, now is it oute.
I myghte no lenger kepe it, out of doute."

- Why did Chaucer choose to include the digression into Midas' tale?
- The fairy tale elements are very strong in lines 983 onwards: dancers who magically disappear; an old, wise woman left behind, offering help in the nick of time. Discuss with a partner whether you feel that there is anything about the knight or the old woman in these lines to make the reader aware that this is still very much the Wife's story.

| | |
|---|---|
| 979 | **thogh we a time abide** even if we wait a while |
| 980 | **out it moot** it must come out |
| 982 | **leere** learn |
| 986 | **the goost** the soul, spirit |
| 987 | **sojourne** stay longer |
| 989-92 | **in his wey ... yet mo** it happened that his road took him by a forest edge, where he saw twenty four ladies, or even more, performing a dance |
| 993 | **drow ful yerne** eagerly drew near |
| 996 | **he niste where** he knew not where |
| 997 | **that bar lyf** that was living |
| 999 | **A fouler ... devise** no man could imagine an uglier creature |
| 1000 | **Again the knight this olde wyf gan rise** the old woman rose, turning towards the knight |
| 1001 | **heer forth ne lith no wey** there is no way through here |
| 1003 | **paraventure** perhaps |
| 1004 | **kan muchel thing** know a great deal |
| 1005 | **leeve mooder** dear mother [term of respect for old woman] |
| 1006 | **I nam but deed, but if ...** I'm a dead man unless |
| 1008 | **me wisse** tell me |
| | **quite youre hire** reward you |

*Her story reveals that women cannot keep secrets – she tells her audience to read the ending in Ovid's book if they wish. The knight, his quest uncompleted, turns disconsolately for home. He sees a group of dancers, who vanish, leaving him with an old hag, who offers help.*

Heere may ye se, thogh we a time abide,
Yet out it moot; we kan no conseil hide.                    980
The remenant of the tale if ye wol heere,
Redeth Ovide, and ther ye may it leere.
　This knight, of which my tale is specially,
Whan that he saugh he mighte nat come therby—
This is to seye, what wommen love moost—                 985
Withinne his brest ful sorweful was the goost.
But hoom he gooth, he mighte nat sojourne;
The day was come that homward moste he tourne.
And in his wey it happed him to ride,
In al this care, under a forest side,                      990
Wher as he saugh upon a daunce go
Of ladies foure and twenty, and yet mo;
Toward the whiche daunce he drow ful yerne,
In hope that som wisdom sholde he lerne.
But certeinly, er he cam fully there,                      995
Vanisshed was this daunce, he niste where.
No creature saugh he that bar lyf,
Save on the grene he saugh sittinge a wyf;
A fouler wight ther may no man devise.
Again the knight this olde wyf gan rise,                   1000
And seyde, "Sire knight, heer forth ne lith no wey.
Tel me what that ye seken, by youre fey!
Paraventure it may the bettre be;
Thise olde folk kan muchel thing," quod she.
　"My leeve mooder," quod this knight, "certeyn   1005
I nam but deed, but if that I kan seyn
What thing it is that wommen moost desire.
Koude ye me wisse, I wolde wel quite youre hire."

- To plight a troth is to make the most solemn type of promise. By doing this the knight is putting himself entirely at the mercy of the old hag, just as he was formerly at the mercy of the queen. If this tale represents the Wife of Bath's view of the world, consider how much power and influence the female characters possess, and also, how their power is achieved.
- The knight has been seeking an answer, and by getting so many has found none. Look at what he promises the old hag, and why he does so.

| | | | |
|---|---|---|---|
| 1009 | **Plight me ... myn hand** take my hand and give me your word | 1030 | **was bode appeere** was ordered to step forward |
| 1014 | **dar me wel avante** I am quite confident | 1034 | **ne stood nat stille as doth a best** did not stand silent like a dumb ox |
| 1017-9 | **Lat se ... I shal thee teche** show me any woman, be she the grandest of all, be she a fine lady in a headdress, or a townswoman in a coverchief; not one can deny the truth of my words | 1036 | **vois** voice |
| | | 1038 | **sovereinetee** sovereignty, dominion |
| | | 1039 | **As wel over hir housbond as hir love** over her husband, as well as her lover [According to the conventions of courtship a woman could have power over her lover until he became her husband – at which time he took control.] |
| 1021 | **Tho rowned she a pistel** then she whispered a message | | |
| 1022 | **fere** fear | | |
| 1024 | **he had holde his day, as he hadde hight** he had kept to his day as he had promised | | |
| | | 1040 | **maistrie** mastery |
| 1027 | **for that they been wise** for widows are considered to be wise | 1042 | **dooth as yow list** do as you please |

*In return for her help, the knight promises to grant the hag whatever favour she might ask of him.*
*She returns with him to court, where he gives the answer to the queen's question.*

"Plight me thy trouthe heere in myn hand," quod she,
"The nexte thing that I requere thee,                    1010
Thou shalt it do, if it lie in thy might,
And I wol telle it yow er it be night."
    "Have heer my trouthe," quod the knight, "I grante."
    "Thanne," quod she, "I dar me wel avante
Thy lyf is sauf; for I wol stonde therby,               1015
Upon my lyf, the queene wol seye as I.
Lat se which is the proudeste of hem alle,
That wereth on a coverchief or a calle,
That dar seye nay of that I shal thee teche.
Lat us go forth, withouten lenger speche."              1020
Tho rowned she a pistel in his ere,
And bad him to be glad, and have no fere.
    Whan they be comen to the court, this knight
Seyde he had holde his day, as he hadde hight,
And redy was his answere, as he sayde.                  1025
Ful many a noble wyf, and many a maide,
And many a widwe, for that they been wise,
The queene hirself sittinge as a justise,
Assembled been, his answere for to heere;
And afterward this knight was bode appeere.             1030
    To every wight comanded was silence,
And that the knight sholde telle in audience
What thing that worldly wommen loven best.
This knight ne stood nat stille as doth a best,
But to his questioun anon answerde                      1035
With manly vois, that al the court it herde:
    "My lige lady, generally," quod he,
"Wommen desiren to have sovereinetee
As wel over hir housbond as hir love,
And for to been in maistrie him above.                  1040
This is youre mooste desir, thogh ye me kille.
Dooth as yow list; I am heer at youre wille."

81

• Write a report of these events at the queen's court as if you were one of the bystanders. Alternatively, you may wish to imagine you were the hapless knight himself.

| | |
|---|---|
| 1044 | **that contraried that he saide** who denied the truth of what he said |
| 1045 | **han his lyf** to have his life saved |
| 1046 | **up stirte** up jumped |
| 1049 | **er that youre court depart** before your court is dismissed |
| 1056-7 | **For wel thou … upon thy fey!** for you know well I have saved your life; if I lie, then contradict me upon your faith |
| 1058 | **Allas and weilawey** alas and woe is me |
| 1059 | **biheste** promise |
| 1060-1 | **as chees a … my body go** do choose a new request – take all my wealth, but set my body free |

| | |
|---|---|
| 1062-6 | **I shrewe us … and eek thy love** I curse us both! Although I am ugly and old and poor I refuse [your request] – not for all the rare metal and ore under the earth, nor for all the wealth that lies above do I wish for anything other than to be your wife, and also your beloved |
| 1067 | **dampnacioun** damnation |
| 1068 | **nacioun** family, status |
| 1069 | **foule disparaged** so dreadfully shamed |
| 1071 | **constreined was** he was forced |
| | **nedes moste** needs must |
| 1072 | **gooth to bedde** go to bed [always a very important aspect of marriage to the Wife of Bath] |

*All the women agree with his answer, but before he goes the old hag demands that he keeps his promise to her, granting her whatever she wants. To his dismay she wishes to marry him, and he is forced to grant her request.*

---

In al the court ne was ther wyf, ne maide,
Ne widwe, that contraried that he saide,
But seyden he was worthy han his lyf.                    1045
And with that word up stirte the olde wyf,
Which that the knight saugh sittinge on the grene:
"Mercy," quod she, "my soverein lady queene!
Er that youre court departe, do me right.
I taughte this answere unto the knight;                   1050
For which he plighte me his trouthe there,
The firste thing that I wolde him requere,
He wolde it do, if it lay in his might.
Bifore the court thanne preye I thee, sir knight,"
Quod she, "that thou me take unto thy wyf;               1055
For wel thou woost that I have kept they lyf.
If I seye fals, sey nay, upon thy fey!"
   This knight answerde, "Allas, and weilawey!
I woot right wel that swich was my biheste.
For Goddes love, as chees a newe requeste;              1060
Taak al my good, and lat my body go."
   "Nay, thanne," quod she, "I shrewe us bothe two!
For thogh that I be foul, and oold, and poore,
I nolde for al the metal, ne for oore,
That under erthe is grave, or lith above,                1065
But if thy wyf I were, and eek thy love."
   "My love?" quod he, "nay, my dampnacioun!
Allas, that any of my nacioun
Sholde evere so foule disparaged be!"
But al for noght; the ende is this, that he              1070
Constreined was, he nedes moste hire wedde;
And taketh his olde wyf, and gooth to bedde.

- The knight is appalled by his marriage because the old hag is inferior in ways which seem to him to be highly important, particularly in a society in which the ownership of a beautiful, young, well-bred bride is seen as a status symbol. Is he right to be so distressed? Does she bring other attributes to the marriage? Does she deserve him? Why does she want to marry such a feeble-witted example of manhood? Do any of these considerations matter, since after all the whole tale is clearly mere fantasy? Chaucer's audience would expect stories to contain some sort of 'lesson'. Can you discover such a lesson here?
- Consider how effectively Chaucer uses conversation on this page to accentuate the characters and add to the humour.

| | | | |
|---|---|---|---|
| 1074 | **for my necligence I do no cure** in my carelessness I have not bothered | 1086 | **everemo** all the time |
| | | 1087 | *benedicitee!* God save us! |
| 1075 | **th'array** the preparations | 1088 | **Fareth every knight thus with his wyf as ye?** do all knights behave so with their wives? |
| 1079 | **ther nas but** there was only | | |
| 1080 | **prively** secretly | | |
| | **on the morwe** the next day | 1090 | **dangerous** hard to please |
| 1081 | **as an owle** like an owl [a bird rarely seen by day] | 1093 | **certes, yet ne dide I yow nevere unright** certainly, I never did you any wrong |
| 1083 | **in his thoght** in his mind | | |
| 1084 | **abedde ybroght** brought to bed [Part of the wedding celebration was to escort man and wife ceremoniously to the marriage bed, often with loud music and raucous jokes – compare the modern practice of seeing newly-weds off on their honeymoon.] | 1094 | **fare** behave |
| | | 1096 | **gilt** my misdeed |
| | | 1097 | **amended** put right |
| | | 1100 | **loothly** ugly |
| | | 1101 | **so lough a kinde** you are so low-born |
| | | 1102 | **winde** roll about |
| 1085 | **he walweth and he turneth** he tossed and turned | 1103 | **So wolde God myn herte wolde breste!** I wish to God my heart would burst! |

*After a gloomy wedding the knight hides himself away for shame. On the wedding night he tosses and turns in bed, until his old wife sweetly asks him what is wrong. He tells her she is the problem, because of her age, her looks and her low status.*

Now wolden som men seye, paraventure,
That for my necligence I do no cure
To tellen yow the joye and al th'array          1075
That at the feeste was that ilke day.
To which thing shortly answeren I shal:
I seye ther nas no joye ne feeste at al;
Ther nas but hevinesse and muche sorwe.
For prively he wedded hire on the morwe,         1080
And al day after hidde him as an owle,
So wo was him, his wyf looked so foule.
  Greet was the wo the knight hadde in his thoght,
Whan he was with his wyf abedde ybroght;
He walweth and he turneth to and fro.            1085
His olde wyf lay smilinge everemo,
And seyde, "O deere housbonde, *benedicitee!*
Fareth every knight thus with his wyf as ye?
Is this the lawe of King Arthures hous?
Is every knight of his so dangerous?             1090
I am youre owene love and eek youre wyf;
I am she which that saved hath your lyf,
And, certes, yet ne dide I yow nevere unright;
Why fare ye thus with me this firste night?
Ye faren lyk a man had lost his wit.             1095
What is my gilt? For Goddes love, tel me it,
And it shal been amended, if I may."
  "Amended?" quod this knight, "allas, nay, nay!
It wol nat been amended nevere mo.
Thou art so loothly, and so oold also,           1100
And therto comen of so lough a kinde,
That litel wonder is thogh I walwe and winde.
So wolde God myn herte wolde breste!"

'Gentillesse' was a concept as difficult to pin down as the idea of class distinction is today. The word embraces such ideals as courtliness, nobility and honourable behaviour. 'Gentillesse' was expected of the knightly class, since knights traditionally vowed to behave honourably, defending all Christian virtues. 'Lewd' folk (commoners) were assumed to behave coarsely, and with less self-control.

- Look closely at the style and content of this debate on 'gentillesse', which does much to explain what the word stands for. Chaucer has given the whole question an extra dimension here, by suggesting that God is the noblest ancestor it is possible to have – and He is common to us all. Most of the Wife's Tale seems very appropriate to its teller – does this particular section seem different?

| | | | |
|---|---|---|---|
| 1105 | **no wonder is** and no wonder | 1119 | **heritage** inheritance |
| 1107 | **if that me liste** if I chose | 1120 | **heigh parage** noble birth [a distinction between rich family and true gentility is made here] |
| 1108 | **So wel ye mighte bere yow unto me** so that you might then behave far better towards me | | |
| | | 1121 | **biquethe** bequeath |
| 1109 | **But, for ye speken ...** now, because you talk about [the old wife begins her argument] | | **for no thing** in any way [note use of emphatic negatives] |
| | | 1124 | **bad us folwen hem in swich degree** entreated us to behave in the same way |
| 1110 | **old richesse** old money [families considered noble because of established wealth] | | |
| | | 1126 | **that highte Dant** whose name is Dante [Dante lived from 1265 to 1321; Chaucer agreed with many of the Italian poet's ideas, although the Wife of Bath is unlikely to have done so.] |
| 1112 | **nat worth a hen** worthless [*literally:* not worth a hen] | | |
| 1113 | **looke who ...** whoever | | |
| 1114 | **privee and apert** privately and publicly | | |
| | **moost entendeth ay** always tries the most diligently | 1128-30 | **Ful selde ... oure gentillesse** man's moral excellence rarely spreads by virtue of his own ancestry alone; for God wishes us rather to claim our noble status from our origin in Him |
| 1116 | **grettest** greatest | | |
| 1117 | **Crist wole ... oure gentillesse** Christ wants us to recognise that our ability to act nobly stems from our creation by God | | |
| | | 1132 | **temporel** temporal, worldly [as opposed to spiritual] |
| | | | **maime** maim, injure |
| 1118 | **eldres** ancestors | | |

*If he listens to her, says the old wife, she can make things seem better. Beginning with a lecture on*
*'gentillesse' she examines all his objections to her suitability as his bride.*

"Is this," quod she, "the cause of youre unreste?"
"Ye, certeinly," quod he, "no wonder is."                          1105
"Now, sire," quod she, "I koude amende al this,
If that me liste, er it were dayes thre,
So wel ye mighte bere yow unto me.
   But, for ye speken of swich gentillesse
As is descended out of old richesse,                              1110
That therfore sholden ye be gentil men,
Swich arrogance is nat worth an hen.
Looke who that is moost vertuous alway,
Privee and apert, and moost entendeth ay
To do the gentil dedes that he kan;                               1115
Taak him for the grettest gentil man.
Crist wole we claime of him oure gentillesse,
Nat of oure eldres for hire old richesse.
For thogh they yeve us al hir heritage,
For which we claime to been of heigh parage,                      1120
Yet may they nat biquethe, for no thing,
To noon of us hir vertuous living,
That made hem gentil men ycalled be,
And bad us folwen hem in swich degree.
   Wel kan the wise poete of Florence,                            1125
That highte Dant, speken in this sentence.
Lo, in swich maner rym is Dantes tale:
'Ful selde up riseth by his branches smale
Prowesse of man, for God, of his goodnesse,
Wole that of him we claime oure gentillesse';                     1130
For of oure eldres may we no thing claime
But temporel thing, that man may hurte and maime.

Chaucer admired the writings of the Roman philosopher, Boethius, and translated his *De Consolatione Philosophiae* into English. The theories expressed here about the changeability of mankind (as opposed to the unchangeable qualities of virtue itself and of natural elements, such as fire) come from this source.

1134-7 **If gentillesse ... faire office** if gentillesse were naturally implanted in a particular family, passed on from generation to generation, then members of that family would never cease to do noble and virtuous deeds

1139 **Taak fyr and ber it** take fire, and shut it in

**derkeste** darkest

1140 **mount of Kaukasous** Caucasian mountains [to Boethius the furthest point from Rome]

1141 **shette the dores and go thenne** shut the doors and go away

1144 **his office natureel** [The argument is a simple one – fire can't help behaving like fire, whether anyone sees it or not. But men do not always behave with gentillesse, even if they come from 'gentil' families. There is also a suggestion that men appear noble superficially, but lack intrinsic virtue.]

1146 **genterie** gentility

1147 **nat annexed** not necessarily linked to

1148-9 **Sith folk ... in his kinde** since people do not always behave according to the qualities that are attributed to their noble birth

1152 **wole han pris** wishes to be respected

1155-7 **And nel himselven ... duc or erl** if he himself fails to behave like a gentleman, and does not follow the example of his noble ancestor, now dead, he cannot be called 'gentil' himself, even if he is a duke or an earl [Chaucer is most emphatic over this point.]

1158 **vileyns sinful dedes make a cherl** a man is churlish through his deeds not by chance of birth [churls' and 'vileyns' were the lowest class of medieval society]

1159 **renomee** renown, fame

1160 **heigh bountee** great virtue

1161 **a strange thing to thy persone** quite a separate thing from your own personality

1163-4 **Thanne comth ... oure place** so true gentillesse comes from God's grace, and in no way is it inherited from our ancestors

*The old woman pursues her argument on the nature of 'gentillesse', saying that it cannot be considered a natural attribute of so-called 'noble' families.*

Eek every wight woot this as wel as I,
If gentillesse were planted natureelly
Unto a certeyn linage doun the line,                    1135
Privee and apert, thanne wolde they nevere fine
To doon of gentillesse the faire office;
They mighte do no vileynie or vice.
   Taak fyr, and ber it in the derkeste hous
Bitwix this and the mount of Kaukasous,                 1140
And lat men shette the dores and go thenne;
Yet wole the fyr as faire lie and brenne
As twenty thousand men mighte it biholde;
His office natureel ay wol it holde,
Up peril of my lyf, til that it die.                    1145
   Heere may ye se wel how that genterie
Is nat annexed to possessioun,
Sith folk ne doon hir operacioun
Alwey, as dooth the fyr, lo, in his kinde.
For, God it woot, men may wel often finde               1150
A lordes sone do shame and vileynie;
And he that wole han pris of his gentrie,
For he was boren of a gentil hous,
And hadde his eldres noble and vertuous,
And nel himselven do no gentil dedis,                   1155
Ne folwen his gentil auncestre that deed is,
He nis nat gentil, be he duc or erl;
For vileyns sinful dedes make a cherl.
Thy gentillesse nis but renomee
Of thine auncestres, for hire heigh bountee,            1160
Which is a strange thing to thy persone.
For gentillesse cometh fro God allone.
Thanne comth oure verray gentillesse of grace;
It was no thing biquethe us with oure place.

- Traditional thinking considered that woman symbolised flesh, while man symbolised reason. In this section of the Tale (which does not appear in other versions of this well-known story) Chaucer has reversed these roles: the knight, succumbing to fleshly desires, has raped a maiden, whilst the old hag here speaks with the voice of reason, derived directly from God. What effect does this have on the whole feminist/anti-feminist argument?

- What is the meaning of the modern phrase 'a real gentleman'? Who might use such a phrase?

- The discussion of poverty is briefer, and may also seem out of keeping with what we know of the Wife of Bath. Summarise the advantages of poverty listed in lines 1177-1206. Is this a convincing argument? Is it meant to be?

| | |
|---|---|
| 1165 | **Valerius** [Jankin mentioned this author in line 671. Valerius wrote of Tullius Hostillius, legendary king of Rome, and a common herdsman by birth. Seneca and Boethius support the idea of nobility coming from virtuous behaviour.] |
| 1169 | **no drede is** beyond dispute |
| 1170 | **gentil dedis** noble deeds |
| 1171 | **leeve housbonde** dear husband |
| 1172 | **al were it** although |
| 1175-6 | **Thanne am I ... weive sinne** I shall be a gentlewoman when I can live in virtue, avoiding sin |
| 1177 | **me repreeve** reprove me [for my poverty] |
| 1178 | **hye God** God above |
| 1179 | **In wilful poverte chees to live his lyf** chose to live his life as a poor man |

| | |
|---|---|
| 1182 | **a vicious living** a wicked way of life |
| 1184 | **This wole ... clerkes seyn** this is the view Seneca and other scholars support |
| 1185 | **halt him paid** considers himself contented |
| 1186 | **al hadde he nat a sherte** even if he has no shirt to his back |
| 1187 | **coveiteth** envies others |
| 1190 | **knave** a beggar, a low person |
| 1191 | **singeth properly** rejoices in its own nature |
| 1192 | **Juvenal** [a Roman satirist] |
| 1193-4 | **The povre ... singe and pleye** a poor man travelling may sing and dance before thieves, because he possesses nothing worth stealing |

*Tullius Hostillius was a Roman of humblest origins, who rose to the noblest heights. The old woman says she hopes through Christian living to achieve the status of a gentlewoman in God's eyes. She then tackles the knight's complaint that she is poor.*

Thenketh hou noble, as seith Valerius, 1165
Was thilke Tullius Hostillius,
That out of poverte roos to heigh noblesse.
Reedeth Senek, and redeth eek Boece;
Ther shul ye seen expres that it no drede is
That he is gentil that dooth gentil dedis. 1170
And therfore, leeve housbonde, I thus conclude:
Al were it that mine auncestres were rude,
Yet may the hye God, and so hope I,
Grante me grace to liven vertuously.
Thanne am I gentil, whan that I biginne 1175
To liven vertuously and weive sinne.
    And ther as ye of poverte me repreeve,
The hye God, on whom that we bileeve,
In wilful poverte chees to live his lyf.
And certes every man, maiden, or wyf, 1180
May understonde that Jhesus, hevene king,
Ne wolde nat chese a vicious living.
Glad poverte is an honest thing, certeyn;
This wole Senec and othere clerkes seyn.
Whoso that halt him paid of his poverte, 1185
I holde him riche, al hadde he nat a sherte.
He that coveiteth is a povre wight,
For he wolde han that is nat in his might;
But he that noght hath, ne coveiteth have,
Is riche, although ye holde him but a knave. 1190
Verray poverte, it singeth proprely;
Juvenal seith of poverte mirily:
'The povre man, whan he goth by the weye,
Bifore the theves he may singe and pleye.'

- The old woman wastes little time on the problems of age and ugliness and her comments seem much in keeping with what the Wife herself might have felt. However, after this long lecture, she gives her young husband his final crucial test. It is an important one, in the terms of the Wife of Bath's attitude to marriage and husbands, and differs somewhat from the traditional folk tale from which Chaucer adapted this story. Before you look at the young man's answer, discuss with a partner which option seems preferable to you.

| | | | |
|---|---|---|---|
| 1195 | **hateful good** a painful blessing [spiritually uplifting, though physically uncomfortable] | 1207 | **elde** old age |
| | | 1210 | **doon favour** behave with great respect |
| 1196 | **ful greet bringere-out of bisinesse** it makes one work hard | 1211 | **clepe him fader** call an old person father [the neutral term for an old person] |
| 1197 | **greet amendere eek of sapience** it also does wonders for a person's intelligence | 1214 | **drede you ... cokewold** you need not fear that you will be made a cuckold |
| 1199 | **alenge** miserable | 1215-6 | **filthe and ... chastitee** ugliness and old age, I promise you, are great preservers of chastity |
| 1200 | **no wight wol chalenge** no one wishes to own it | | |
| 1203 | **a spectacle** an eyeglass | 1217 | **youre delit** what you really long for |
| | **as thinketh me** it seems to me | 1219 | **tweye** two |
| 1204 | **he may his verray freendes see** through which a man may see his true friends | 1224-5 | **take youre aventure ... cause of me** and take your chance on the amount of traffic in and out of your house on my account |
| 1205 | **sin that I noght yow greve** since I give you nothing to be unhappy about | 1227 | **wheither that yow liketh** whichever you please |

92

*More points in favour of poverty are listed. The old woman then deals with the advantages of an ugly, aged wife, and finally gives her young husband a crucial choice to make.*

Poverte is hateful good and, as I gesse,         1195
A ful greet bringere-out of bisinesse;
A greet amendere eek of sapience
To him that taketh it in pacience.
Poverte is this, although it seme alenge,
Possessioun that no wight wol chalenge.        1200
Poverte ful ofte, whan a man is lowe,
Maketh his God and eek himself to knowe.
Poverte a spectacle is, as thinketh me,
Thurgh which he may his verray freendes see.
And therefore, sire, sin that I noght yow greve,     1205
Of my poverte namoore ye me repreve.
   Now, sire, of elde ye repreve me;
And certes, sire, thogh noon auctoritee
Were in no book, ye gentils of honour
Seyn that men sholde an oold wight doon favour,    1210
And clepe him fader, for youre gentillesse;
And auctours shal I finden, as I gesse.
   Now ther ye seye that I am foul and old,
Than drede you noght to been a cokewold;
For filthe and eelde, also moot I thee,          1215
Been grete wardeyns upon chastitee.
But nathelees, sin I knowe youre delit,
I shal fulfille youre worldly appetit.
   Chese now," quod she, "oon of thise thinges tweye:
To han me foul and old til that I deye,         1220
And be to yow a trewe, humble wyf,
And nevere yow displese in al my lyf;
Or elles ye wol han me yong and fair,
And take youre aventure of the repair
That shal be to youre hous by cause of me,      1225
Or in som oother place, may wel be.
Now chese yourselven, wheither that yow liketh."

- Look carefully at the contract made between the knight and his old wife in lines 1230-49. What has changed? What do you think the knight has learnt about dealing with women?
- It is quite clear that this is the perfect ending from the Wife of Bath's point of view. Look at the similarity between the knight's words here and those of Jankin after his defeat. Does the knight deserve such a reward? Does the ending of the tale suggest anything about the storyteller's own wishful thinking? Is it true that husbands only have to be submissive and obedient for their wives to be perfectly angelic?

| Line | Gloss |
|---|---|
| 1228 | **aviseth him** considered carefully |
| | **sore siketh** sighed bitterly |
| 1231 | **youre wise governance** your wise control |
| 1232-3 | **moost plesance ... and me also** most pleasure and honour to you, and to me as well |
| 1234 | **I do no fors the wheither** I do not care which of the two |
| 1236 | **maistrie** mastery, control |
| 1237 | **as me lest** as I please |
| 1239 | **wrothe** angry |
| 1241 | **ye** yes |
| 1242 | **I prey ... sterven wood / But** May God let me die insane unless |
| 1245 | **and but I be** and unless I am |
| 1246 | **emperice** empress |
| 1249 | **Cast up the curtin** lift the curtain [the curtain around the bed] |
| 1252 | **hente hire** he clasped her |
| 1254 | **a-rewe** one after another |

*The knight chooses and receives an unexpected reward. The fairy tale ends happily ever after.*

This knight aviseth him and sore siketh,
But atte laste he seyde in this manere:
"My lady and my love, and wyf so deere,      1230
I put me in youre wise governance;
Cheseth youreself which may be moost plesance,
And moost honour to yow and me also.
I do no fors the wheither of the two;
For as yow liketh, it suffiseth me."      1235
   "Thanne have I gete of yow maistrie," quod she,
"Sin I may chese and governe as me lest?"
   "Ye, certes, wyf," quod he, "I holde it best."
   "Kis me," quod she, "we be no lenger wrothe;
For, by my trouthe, I wol be to yow bothe,      1240
This is to seyn, ye, bothe fair and good.
I prey to God that I moote sterven wood,
But I to yow be also good and trewe
As evere was wyf, sin that the world was newe.
And but I be to-morn as fair to seene      1245
As any lady, emperice, or queene,
That is bitwixe the est and eke the west,
Dooth with my lyf and deth right as yow lest.
Cast up the curtin, looke how that it is."
   And whan the knight saugh verraily al this,      1250
That she so fair was, and so yong therto,
For joye he hente hire in his armes two,
His herte bathed in a bath of blisse.
A thousand time a-rewe he gan hire kisse,
And she obeyed him in every thing      1255
That mighte doon him plesance or liking.

- There is no doubt that Chaucer intended his audience to appreciate the fact that his characters see the world from a very subjective viewpoint. The Wife's view of marriage is unlikely to be Chaucer's own, nor is it intended to be the view of all women. In the fourteenth century audiences expected stories to contain some sort of moral truths. What is the moral behind this tale?
- At the end the Wife sees herself as a 'winner' in the game of life. She has 'won' against her old husbands, and found ways to subdue numbers four and five. She has used her tale to get back at the Friar, and she has shown how women may dominate men through the tale she tells. Is she really a winner? Is she likely to be happy and contented? Has her fierce fight against male supremacy made her independent? Is she some comic male nightmare of a woman? These are all questions Chaucer seems to invite us to consider.

| 1257-8 | **unto hir lives ende / In parfit joye** happily ever after |
| 1259 | **meeke, yonge, and fressh abedde** obedient, young and lively in bed |
| 1260 | **grace t'overbide hem that we wedde** God's grace, or luck, to outlive our husbands |
| 1263-4 | **And olde ... verray pestilence!** God send a real plague down on mean old, angry skinflints! |

96

*Her tale is ended, and the Wife hopes that God will send all women fine, young husbands to make them happy – and a plague on the other sort.*

And thus they live unto hir lives ende
In parfit joye; and Jhesu Crist us sende
Housbondes meeke, yonge, and fressh abedde,
And grace t'overbide hem that we wedde;               1260
And eek I praye Jhesu shorte hir lives
That wol nat be governed by hir wives;
And olde and angry nigardes of dispence,
God sende hem soone verray pestilence!'

# The Tale she tells...

The story Chaucer eventually decided to give to the Wife of Bath was one with which his audience would probably be familiar. The 'loathly lady' with magical powers was a well-known folk tale. Chaucer preserved the essence of the story, but added or altered certain significant details, listed below. It is interesting to compare the original with his version, and to decide why he made these changes.

| Folk tale | Chaucer |
|---|---|
| a) The man is a noble youth. | He is a knight of Arthur's table. |
| b) The youth kills an enemy in battle and is taken prisoner. | He rapes a maiden. |
| c) Rules of battle say he cannot be killed, so he is set an impossible question. | The law says he ought to be executed – but his life is saved by the queen. |
| d) The loathly lady tells the youth what she wants as a prize. | Old hag says she'll ask 'a favour'. |
| e) The youth goes to court alone. | Old hag accompanies him. |
| f) Marriage | Wedding night problems and lectures are Chaucer's addition. |
| g) The choice offered is foul by day and fair by night, or the other way round i.e. he could have public or private satisfaction. | The knight is left with no real choice: if 'foul' he will be a laughing stock and thus lose status; if 'fair' she could be unfaithful. So all power lies in her hands. |
| h) The Loathly Lady is freed from a spell by the noble youth's virtue and 'gentillesse'. | The old hag **chooses** to become beautiful, and thus rewards the man for giving her sovereignty. |

# Chaucer's pilgrims

*The Canterbury pilgrims leaving the Tabard Inn at Southwark*

*In order of appearance:*

**The Knight**  brave, devout and unassuming – the perfect gentleman

**The Squire**  in training to follow in the Knight, his father's, footsteps, a fine and fashionable young man, and madly in love

**The Yeoman**  the Knight's only servant, a skilled bowman and forester

**The Prioress**  a most ladylike head of a nunnery; she takes great pains with her appearance and manners; she loves animals. She is accompanied by another nun and three priests, the nun and one priest also telling tales

**The Monk**  fine and prosperous looking, well-mounted; he loves hunting

**The Friar**  cheerful and sociable, he is skilled at obtaining alms from those he visits, particularly the ladies

**The Merchant**  rather secretive; his main interest is commerce

**The Clerk**  thin and shabby, his passion is scholarship; he spends all he has on books

**The Sergeant at Law**  a judge at the assize courts; one of the few pilgrims about whom Chaucer says very little

**The Franklin**  a wealthy and hospitable landowner and a JP; but not a member of the aristocracy

**The Five Guildsmen**  although they pursue different crafts or trades, they belong to the same social guild – rather self-important townsfolk

**The Cook**  he has been brought along to provide meals for the company; although a versatile cook, Chaucer suggests his personal hygiene could be improved

**The Shipman**  a weather-beaten master mariner

| | |
|---|---|
| **The Doctor of Physic** | finely dressed and a skilled medical practitioner; he is an expert in astrology and natural magic; he loves gold |
| **The Wife of Bath** | skilled at weaving; her chief claim to fame is her five husbands |
| **The Parson** | the only truly devout churchman in Chaucer's group; he avoids all the tricks unscrupulous clerics used to get rich, and spends his care and energy on his parishioners |
| **The Ploughman** | the Parson's brother, and, like him, a simple, honest hard-working man |
| **The Miller** | tough, ugly and a cheat |
| **The Manciple** | responsible for organising the provisions for the lawyers in one of the Inns of Court – clearly a plum job for a clever man |
| **The Reeve** | unsociable, but able; the estate manager of a young nobleman |
| **The Summoner** | an official of a church court; corrupt, lewd and offensive |
| **The Pardoner** | another unpleasant churchman – he earns money by selling 'pardons' from Rome, and by letting simple folk see the fake holy relics he carries |
| **The Host** | the genial landlord of 'The Tabard', who accompanies them on the pilgrimage, and organises the story-telling |
| **Geoffrey Chaucer** | he depicts himself as rather shy and unassuming. |

They are later joined by another story teller – **The Canon's Yeoman**, a servant whose tale betrays his master's obsessive interest in alchemy.

*Modern pilgrims attending mass in the cathedral at Compostela, Spain*

# Pilgrims and pilgrimages

Pilgrimages are journeys made to sacred places, usually as acts of religious devotion. They became increasingly popular during the twelfth and thirteenth centuries, at the time when the threats to the Christian world from infidels and heathens from the east reached their height. The passion to defend and reaffirm the power of the Christian church manifested itself in Crusades to the Holy Land, and an upsurge in religious fervour. Shrines were established in many European countries in places of great religious significance. In England, Canterbury Cathedral was the site of the assassination of Archbishop Becket; Walsingham in Norfolk became a holy site of pilgrimage after visions of the Virgin Mary had been seen there. The great cathedral city of Cologne was another centre of pilgrimage, as was Compostela. Further afield, many pilgrims made the long journey to Jerusalem, available for visits from Christian pilgrims after the Emperor Frederick II had negotiated peace with the infidels, and had himself crowned king of the holy city.

Pilgrims (travelling in groups for companionship and safety) would travel to shrines at home and abroad to celebrate their devotion to the church, to seek pardon for their sins, and to ask favours of the saint whose relics were preserved in that place. The traditional image of a pilgrim is of one who travels humbly and simply, dressed in plain clothes, often on foot, carrying a staff. The emblem of a pilgrim is the scallop or cockle shell, worn on cap or hood. This was particularly the symbol of St James, patron saint of military crusaders, and the journey to his shrine in Compostela, northern Spain, was, and still is, one of the great pilgrim routes across Europe. The shells may originally have been real ones, but were later moulded in lead, as were most other pilgrim badges.

By the time Chaucer decided to use a group of pilgrims as a framework for his *Canterbury Tales*, reasons for pilgrimage had become less exclusively devotional. It was certainly a profitable business for enterprising people, as well as a popular pastime. The tourist industry began to take off. The Venetians offered a regular ferry service carrying travellers to and from the Holy Land. The monks of Cluny, the greatest religious house in France, ran a string of hotels along the entire route between their monastery and Compostela. Travel guides were produced, giving information about accommodation available along the route. One for Compostela contained useful Basque vocabulary, and a description of what to see in the cathedral. Horse traders did a healthy trade hiring out horses to pilgrims.

There was great competition for popular relics between the religious establishments, which sometimes led to rather obvious forgeries. At least two places, for instance, claimed to possess the head of John the Baptist. Pilgrims began to bring home their own souvenirs, and to house them in their local churches, like the fourteenth century traveller William Wey, who proudly deposited in his Wiltshire village church his maps, a reproduction of St Veronica's handkerchief, which he had rubbed on the pillars of 'the tempyl of Jerusalem', and a large number of stones picked up in sites around the Holy Land. His parish priest was presumably delighted. Badges and emblems made of lead were sold at shrines, and eagerly purchased as souvenirs by travellers – the cockle shell for St James, the palm tree from Jericho. At Canterbury it was possible to buy an assortment of badges – an image of the head of the saint, St Thomas riding a horse, a little bell, or a small ampulla [bottle] to hold sacred water. Permission was given from Rome for the local religious houses to obtain a licence to manufacture these.

Some of Chaucer's pilgrims seem to have genuinely devout reasons for visiting Canterbury: the Knight, for instance, has come straight from his military expeditions abroad, fighting for Christendom, and his simple coat is still stained from its contact with his coat of mail. On the other hand, the Wife of Bath, although an enthusiastic pilgrim, hardly seems to be travelling in a spirit of piety or devotion. She lists the places she has visited like a seasoned traveller determined to visit as many tourist attractions as possible. By using a pilgrimage as the frame on which to hang his stories and characterisations, Chaucer was able to point out the way in which attitudes and standards were changing and old values were being lost.

*Geoffrey Chaucer*

# Geoffrey Chaucer

## BIOGRAPHICAL NOTES

**1340?**   The actual date of his birth is uncertain, but he was near 60 when he died. His father and grandfather were both vintners – wealthy London merchants, who supplied wines to the king's court.

Chaucer was introduced to court life in his teens. By the age of 16 he was employed in the service of the wife of the king's son, Lionel, later Duke of Clarence.

**1359**   He fought in France in the army of Edward III. He was captured and imprisoned, but released on payment of his ransom by the duke.

Chaucer was clearly valued by the king himself and other members of the powerful royal family. In the **1360s** and **1370s** he was sent abroad on diplomatic missions to France, Genoa, Florence and Lombardy.

**1360s**   He married Philippa de Roet, daughter of Sir Paon de Roet of Hainault, and maid-in-waiting to Edward III's wife, Queen Philippa, also from Hainault. Philippa Chaucer's half-sister was Katherine Swynford, originally nurse and governess to John of Gaunt's children by his first wife, the Lady Blanche, subsequently his mistress, and ultimately his third wife. The link with this powerful Duke of Lancaster was an important one: the duke was Chaucer's patron and friend, in later life giving Chaucer a pension of £10 a year.

**1370?**   Chaucer wrote *The Boke of the Duchess*.

**1374**   The position of Comptroller of Customs for the Port of London was given to Chaucer, and in the same year the king granted him a pitcher of wine daily. Other lucrative posts in the administration of customs became his later.

**1374**   Chaucer began his unfinished work *The House of Fame*.

**1382**   Chaucer wrote *The Parlement of Fowles* – possibly for Richard II's marriage.

**1386**   Like the Franklin in *The Canterbury Tales*, Chaucer was appointed 'Knight of the Shire' or Parliamentary representative for the county of Kent.

**1385-8** He wrote *Troilus and Criseyde*.

It seems that, in spite of the royal and noble patronage he enjoyed, Chaucer was an extravagant man, and money slipped through his fingers. In 1389 he was appointed Clerk of the King's Works by Richard II, but the position lasted only two years. It may be that the poet lost his official position and favour during the political upheavals of Richard's reign. Richard later gave him a pension of £20 for life, which Chaucer frequently asked for 'in advance'. Threats of arrest for non-payment of debts were warded off by letters of protection from the crown.

**1388**   Chaucer went on a pilgrimage, possibly formulating his ideas for *The Canterbury Tales*.

**1391**   He spent some time in Petherton, Somerset, as deputy forester.

**1399** Henry IV, son of John of Gaunt, became king, and Chaucer was awarded a new pension of 40 marks (about £26), which allowed him to live his few remaining months in comfort.

**1400** Chaucer died in October, and was buried in Westminster Abbey.

## CHAUCER THE WRITER AND SCHOLAR

Although Geoffrey Chaucer was actively involved in diplomatic life, moving in court circles, and travelling extensively, he was also an extremely well-read man. His own works show the influence of classical writers, as well as more recent French and Italian works. The wide range of biblical, classical and contemporary literary references in the Wife's Prologue and Tale bear witness to his 'bookishness', and he confesses to owning 60 books – a very considerable library in those days. Many of the ideas and themes which occur in *The Canterbury Tales* have been adapted from the works of classical and contemporary sources known to Chaucer and to at least some of his audiences.

Some of his best known works have been mentioned above. His earliest works, such as *The Boke of the Duchess*, show the influence of the French romances, for example the works of twelfth-century Marie de France, and the *Roman de la Rose*. Chaucer's work is a dream-poem in this tradition, and a lament for the death of the beautiful Blanche of Lancaster, John of Gaunt's first wife.

*The House of Fame*, an unfinished narrative poem, suggests both French and Italian influences. In this poem the dreamer meets various categories of famous people, rather as Dante (1265-1321) presents his categories in the *Inferno*. Chaucer admired Dante's works, as well as the writings of two other Italians, Petrarch and Boccaccio, both of whom he is reputed to have met whilst on diplomatic business in Italy. In fact, Boccaccio's *Decameron*, written forty years or so before *The Canterbury Tales*, employs the linking device (in his case a group of sophisticated men and women, entertaining one another with story-telling in a country retreat, whilst the Black Death rages in Florence) that Chaucer was to use later with far greater subtlety, variety and skill.

In *Troilus and Criseyde*, Chaucer's re-telling of the tale of love and betrayal at the time of the Trojan Wars, he shows his debt to classical writers. It is considered to be one of his best works. *The Canterbury Tales* are full of allusions to the works of Homer, Horace, Virgil, Ovid and Plato, as well as references to Old and New Testament stories. Chaucer showed a scholarly understanding of the writings of many theologians respected in the Middle Ages, such as St Jerome and St Augustine. He greatly admired the Roman philosopher Boethius, and translated his work *De Consolatione Philosophiae* from the Latin original into English. He clearly had an interest in astronomy and astrology (notice the Wife of Bath's insistence on the effect of the planets on her personality) and wrote *A Treatise on the Astrolabe*, explaining the workings of this astronomical instrument, which he dedicated *to little Lewise*, his young son, who died in childhood.

These are just some of the best known of Chaucer's own writings, and give some idea of the breadth and depth of his scholarship and interests.

# Marriage or virginity?

## THE BIBLICAL CASE FOR VIRGINITY

*(The line references below are to the Wife of Bath's Prologue.)*

The 'wo that is in mariage' is a subject often referred to by St Paul in his letters. The Wife refers extensively to Paul's first letter to the Corinthians, particularly Chapter 7, in which he discusses the question of marriage versus virginity at some length. As a virgin himself, he feels that bringing man and woman together is bound to lead to trouble (verse 1; **line 87**). Nevertheless, if they feel they must live together, then marriage is better than living in sin (verses 2 and 3). A marriage in which husband and wife do not have sex together is something he approves of (verse 5; **lines 93-4**). Paul admits (verse 6) that God has never commanded virginity, but it is a way of life that the apostle strongly recommends (**line 65**). He would like everyone to be a virgin like him (verse 7) but knows that God has given every man and woman different qualities and virtues (**line 103**). If other men and women can't manage the restraint of virginity, then, he agrees, they are better married than living in sin; but he recommends that those who are still unmarried, or widowed, should follow his own example of virginity (verse 9; referred to by the Wife in **lines 49, 52, 81, 84 and 92**).

Other Biblical 'disapproval' of marriage comes from St John, Chapter 2. In **line 11** of the Prologue there is mention of the wedding in Cana (where Jesus turned water into wine) – the only reference to a wedding visit by Jesus in the Bible. Medieval churchmen, who opposed the idea of remarriage, used this as proof that Jesus intended people to marry only once. John also mentions the occasion when Jesus met a Samaritan beside a well: he told her that she was not truly married to her current partner, since she had had five husbands (St John 4 verses 7-19).

## THE BIBLICAL CASE FOR ONE MARRIAGE (or more than one)

**Line 28** refers to Genesis 1 verse 28.

**Line 30** refers to St Matthew 19 verse 5. Here Matthew reports Jesus's words to the Pharisee: if man and woman have united in marriage then this is a bond blessed by God.

**Line 36** refers to 1 Kings 11 verse 3 – Solomon's 700 wives and 300 concubines. The Wife fails to mention, however, that the Bible goes on to say that they 'turned away his heart' from the Lord.

**Line 54** refers to Lameth, mentioned in Genesis 4 as having two wives, Adah and Zillah.

**Line 101** refers to wooden and clay pots being of use in great houses, as in Paul's second letter to Timothy, Chapter 2 verse 20. Later, **line 145** refers to the barley bread distributed by Jesus as related in the miracle of the loaves and the fishes in St Mark 6 verse 38 and Chapter 8.

In **lines 130** and **156-159** the Wife uses the words of Paul, her greatest critic. In the same chapter of the first letter to the Corinthians mentioned above he states that those who do marry should do their duty to one another – husbands should 'pay their debt' to wives, and wives to husbands. He also says that wives have control over their husbands' bodies; and husbands over wives. The Wife of Bath chooses to edit these texts to suit herself.

# The status of women in the fourteenth century

Chaucer describes only two women among his Canterbury pilgrims, although the Prioress does have another nun travelling with her. Very different from one another in character and behaviour, they nevertheless represent areas of society in which women could achieve considerable power and influence, in a world dominated legally, economically and socially by men.

## VIEWS ON WOMEN

Women were, officially at least, very much the second sex. On the one hand, they were the daughters of Eve. The church taught that Eve had listened to the persuasions of Satan and cajoled Adam into disobeying God's laws. Women were therefore tricky, troublesome and the cause of man's downfall. Marriage was an unfortunate necessity for the majority of men, since it resulted in children – certainly something to be encouraged after the decline in population during the plague years. Legally, a woman became her husband's property on marriage, and her own wealth passed to him. Those who avoided women, however, and embraced more spiritual or intellectual pleasures, were admired as purer and somehow finer.

On the other hand, Christ's mother, Mary, was also a woman, and adoration of the Virgin Mary figured very strongly in late medieval thinking. Men worshipped her as a figure who was both purely virginal and the embodiment of mother-love. So, in her name, women were also to be worshipped and adored, brave deeds and noble ventures being performed in the name of glorious womanhood. The cult of Mary and the courtly love tradition, by which a noble woman was loved and adored from afar, became intertwined. Here, then, are two very distinct views of women, both deriving from church teaching of the time.

With some exceptions, women rarely received an academic education, for, although there were a few grammar schools, these were largely run by monasteries, and offered education to clever boys from poor families, who could eventually become clerks, attached to the monastery. Girls were not welcome. Girls from noble families could attend 'song schools' as young children, but their main education was learning to run a large household – home economics, embroidery, French, singing, dancing and elegant manners were considered sufficient for them. Because more men were literate and 'educated' in the bookish sense they had the 'authority'. At least allegedly so.

## AREAS OF POWER AND INFLUENCE

Of the two areas in which women held their own to an extent, the first was in the church. Wealthy men with too many daughters would offer their surplus to a suitable convent, when they were about 14. In return for a dowry the girls received an education, and fathers were saved the trouble of finding them husbands, for there were no professions open to women in those days. Many nunneries became rather like fashionable ladies' clubs 'not conducive to austerity or zeal'. The most powerful person in the nunnery was unquestionably the Prioress. She was responsible for

*Women at work: collecting wool and weaving*

looking after the business of the estates – often quite extensive – as well as the internal discipline of the house. She entertained any guests who arrived at her doors (and many wealthy women travellers used nunneries as genteel hotels) and she answered to her bishop for the spiritual and earthly welfare of her nuns. Even so, the wealth and standing of these nunneries was not comparable to that of the great monasteries.

The second, much smaller, group contained women of lower social status with some trade skill, such as weaving. By the fourteenth century the cloth industry had increased to such an extent that it overtook the export trade in raw wool. Weaving was a cottage industry, and weavers, often wealthy, and certainly valued workers in their own right, were part of the greatest industry in England. Most weavers were men. It is interesting that, although Chaucer mentions the Wife of Bath's skill at weaving in the General Prologue, there is no further mention of it – as if she achieved her power and position through other means.

Throughout history there is abundant evidence of women achieving power and influence by alternative methods. Books and writers, the church and the law all stated that men were superior in intellect and power. But all around them men and women could see examples of female authority and competence, from the chatelaines who ran the enormous households and estates of their lords, whilst those gentlemen were away crusading, or fighting in France, to the widows or daughters who took over and ran family businesses, and became leather workers, butchers, alehouse owners, weavers. Furthermore, in private life, then as always, relationships between men and women did not necessarily reveal the man as master in his own home. Very often, in the writings, carvings and illustrations of the period, the married woman is depicted as a scold and a tyrant – the boss, in fact. The marriage relationship, in all its varying forms, is one which fascinates Chaucer in *The Canterbury Tales*, nowhere more so than in the Wife's Tale. It is the contradiction between what one is told and what is perceived to be true that the Wife challenges in her life and her Tale.

*This woodcarving shows a woman beating her husband*

# The role of the church

## A CHURCH-DOMINATED SOCIETY

The church exerted its power and influence over all aspects of fourteenth century life.

- Everyone was expected to attend services, make regular confessions and give offerings to the church.
- The only artistic or theatrical experiences most people enjoyed came from brightly coloured church paintings or carvings, church music and lavish ceremonies. They enjoyed dramatic and exciting sermons, often preached by travelling friars, who were practically professional performers.
- Hospitals and schools, where they existed, were run by monasteries, which also offered hospitality to (wealthy) travellers.
- Monastic orders owned vast estates and employed lay workers in their fields, offices, dairies and kitchens. (It has been estimated that only one-third of the population of monasteries were actually monks by the fourteenth century.) In great cathedral towns and cities, such as York and Canterbury, and in the areas around the richest monasteries, the church had extensive control over the population, not just spiritually, but over wages, housing, food supplies – every aspect of secular life. This was so despite the growth of a thriving merchant class in towns and cities.
- The church had real political power. Well into the fourteenth century the position of Chancellor, treasurer of the realm, was a post usually held by a churchman – whose allegiance was not just to his king, but also to the Pope.
- Church law courts had considerable privileges. Members of the clergy could not be tried and sentenced in the law courts set up for the rest of the nation – their own courts gave them considerable protection and privilege, including rights of appeal to the Pope.

## GROWING DISCONTENT

It was inconceivable that such a dominant institution should escape criticism. There was a long tradition of literary satire, already two centuries old by Chaucer's time, and well-established among the French poets he read and admired. Some of Chaucer's own satirical and humorous criticisms of the clerical pilgrims can be seen as part of this literary tradition, which focused largely on two areas of discontent: complaints about church wealth, and complaints about the behaviour of churchmen.

- The Commons declared that one-third of the country's wealth lay in the hands of the church. It was enormously powerful. Even the evangelical orders of travelling friars (originally set up in reaction to the laxity and wealth of the church) had become property-owning institutions, often as rich and worldly as other branches. Critics claimed that greedy churchmen worshipped 'Saints Gold and Silver'.
- Priests urged congregations to lead sober and virtuous lives, but some provided poor examples themselves. Some men became parish priests for the revenue they could obtain, then 'farmed out' the parishes for a pittance to uneducated substi-

tutes. Stories about bad behaviour in monasteries and nunneries were numerous, and widely enjoyed (in the same way as satirical articles and magazines provide entertainment today by attacking the establishment). Original monastic standards of poverty, abstinence, chastity and sober godliness seemed largely forgotten.

*A monk enjoys the contents of the monastic cellar*

## THE CHURCH CHALLENGED

The fourteenth century was a time of considerable upheaval against the long-established tradition of church power. The dominance of the centuries-old church institutions was challenged several times in Chaucer's lifetime.

Political attempts to limit church power were made through statutes or laws:
- In 1351, the First Statute of Provisors put a stop to the Pope's claim to choose clergy for English parishes – an understandable defensive move at the time, since the papal residence was then in Avignon (dangerously close to the territory of England's enemy, France).
- In 1371, the Commons complained that the church had control over the country's wealth, through its influence over the treasury.
- In 1388, the Commons objected to the Pope's influence over the choice of English bishops.

### The Peasants' Revolt

When revolution shook the country in 1381, many of the complaints voiced by its leaders were against the oppressive power of the old landlords, particularly the church.
- The powerful monasteries of the south east were ferociously attacked.
- The rebel leader, Wat Tyler, beheaded the Archbishop of Canterbury on Tower Hill. (He was later to suffer the same fate himself at the hand of the Mayor of London.)

## LOSS OF INFLUENCE

In the fourteenth century the church began to lose some of its extreme influence.

- John Wyclif, the great scholar and philosopher at Oxford University, suggested deep theological reasons why the church should own no property. He believed that academic centres should be free from undue church influence. His followers, known as Lollards, travelled the country, practising an evangelical religion drawn directly from the Bible, newly translated into English.
- The fourteenth century was a time of growth in towns, with their industry and trade. People became more prosperous and settled. Fear of death from the dreaded plague lessened. In this atmosphere, criticism of the church became more vocal and widespread.
- Learning from the techniques which had made the old monastic estates so wealthy, lords and nobles managed their own estates with greater efficiency.
- More people were learning to read and write by going to school – and the church no longer had such a control over educational establishments. For instance, in 1382 the successful William of Wykeham founded a comprehensive school at Winchester, with scholarships to support children as poor as he had been, on the principle that it is 'manners' (not birth) that 'makyth man'.

While it would be wrong, therefore, to read Chaucer's picture of the church as 'the truth and nothing but the truth', there is no doubt that his unforgettable caricatures – the hypocritical friar, the greedy monk – would have been recognised and enjoyed by the successful nobles and self-confident townsmen who formed his audience. That type of churchman belonged to an old economic order, under general attack in the years when Chaucer was writing, and the old order's surrender to a changing society was no doubt sped on its way by *The Canterbury Tales* – and also, perhaps, even more radically, by William Langland's *Piers Plowman*.

*Craftsmen delighted in making fun of church dignitaries*

# Themes in the Wife of Bath

1 **Male/female relationships**
   a) Is it true that women want 'dominance'?
   b) How accurately does Chaucer portray relationships between men and women in both Prologue and Tale? Think about such aspects as the Wife and the Pardoner, the Wife and the Friar, the knight and the maiden, the queen and the knight, the queen and the king – as well as more obvious ones.
   c) Does Chaucer agree with the sentiments of his creation, the Wife, and her views on marriage? How does he enable us to see her in critical and sympathetic ways? Is it possible to guess what he thinks about marriage himself?

2 **Humour**
   a) Are we meant to take the Wife seriously? Does she take herself seriously?
   b) What sorts of humour can you find in this Prologue and Tale – satire? bawdy? characterisation? cut and thrust of wit and argument between characters? absurd situations?
   c) Is the Wife just funny, or is she a monster?

3 **Tale and teller**
   a) Is the Tale appropriate for this teller?
   b) Do we learn more about the Wife from the Tale? What is the significance of her deafness?
   c) Are ideas such as hypocrisy, justice, sex, scholarship, etc. handled similarly in both Prologue and Tale? Does anything (for example, 'gentillesse') seem out of place?
   d) What aspects of storytelling do you discern in both? For example, use of digression, colloquial language, conversation, lively metaphor and simile?

4 **Chaucer's style**
   a) What methods does he use to make the style in keeping with the character of the Wife?
   b) How effectively does the writer create for the reader an idea of medieval life and times?
   c) Is he funny? subtle? lively? learned? descriptive? scholarly? Find examples from the text to illustrate the points you make.
   d) Chaucer was extremely widely read. How far does his own scholarship and literary knowledge add an extra dimension to what he says?

5 **Chaucer and the fourteenth century**
   a) What do we learn about religion and attitudes to it?
   b) How much power did women really have?
   c) Does Chaucer create a really believable character here, or just a stereotype? And can we, today, identify with either?

Use these questions as a basis for written work or class discussion.

# Glossary of frequently-used words

| | | | |
|---|---|---|---|
| abide | wait a moment, stay | maide | virgin (male or female) |
| anon | straight away | maidenhede | virginity |
| axe | ask | mo | more |
| bad | ordered | nathelees | nevertheless |
| breed | bread | nis | is not |
| chese | choose | noght | nothing |
| clepe(d) | name(d) | noon | no, none |
| clerke | scholar (frequently churchman) | pardee | by God (par dieu) |
| | | quod | said |
| conseil(le) | advice, recommendation | seith | says |
| daungerous | grudging, reluctant, difficult to please | sholde | should |
| | | sith | since |
| defended | forbade | sondry | various |
| dorste | dared | sothe/sooth | truth |
| ech | each | stirte | jumps |
| eek | also | swich | such |
| flour | flower | swinke | work |
| freletee | frailty, weakness | thral | slave |
| gentil | noble | trowe | believe |
| glose | interpret, explain, persuade | wight | person |
| | | wiste | knew |
| goost | spirit, soul | wo | misery |
| hem | them | wolde | would, wanted |
| herkne | listen | woot | know, knew |
| hir | their | wrothe | angry |
| hoten | be called | yaf/yeve | give, gave |
| ilke | this here, this same | yifte | gift |
| indulgence | allowance | ywis | you know, indeed, certainly |
| list | choose **if you list** if you like, if it pleases you | | |